Drug Therapy and Dissociative Disorders

Psychiatric Disorders
Drugs and Psychology for the Mind and Body

Drug Therapy and Adjustment Disorders

Drug Therapy and Anxiety Disorders

Drug Therapy and Cognitive Disorders

Drug Therapy and Childhood and Adolescent Disorders

Drug Therapy and Dissociative Disorders

Drug Therapy and Eating Disorders

Drug Therapy and Impulse Control Disorders

Drug Therapy for Mental Disorders Caused by a Medical Condition

Drug Therapy and Mood Disorders

Drug Therapy and Obsessive-Compulsive Disorder

Drug Therapy and Personality Disorders

Drug Therapyand Postpartum Disorders

Drug Therapy and Premenstrual Disorders

Drug Therapy and Psychosomatic Disorders

Drug Therapy and Schizophrenia

Drug Therapy and Sexual Disorders

Drug Therapy and Sleep Disorders

Drug Therapy and Substance-Related Disorders

The FDA and Psychiatric Drugs: How a Drug Is Approved

Psychiatric Disorders:
Drugs and Psychology for the
Mind and Body

Drug Therapy and Dissociative Disorders

BY AUTUMN LIBAL

MASON CREST PUBLISHERS

Mason Crest Publishers Inc.
370 Reed Road
Broomall, Pennsylvania 19008
(866) MCP-BOOK (toll free)

First printing
1 2 3 4 5 6 7 8 9 10
Libal, Autumn.
Drug therapy and dissociative disorders / Autumn Libal.
p. cm.—(Psychiatric disorders: drugs and psychology for the mind and body)
Summary: Examines dissociative disorders, their symptoms and manifestations, how they can be controlled and treated, and what it is like to live with a dissociative disorder. Includes bibliographical references and index.
1. Dissociative disorders—Juvenile literature. 2. Dissociative disorders—Chemotherapy—Juvenile literature. [1. Dissociative disorders.] I. Title. II. Series.
RC553.D5L53 2004
616.85'23061—dc21
2003002381

ISBN 1-59084-564-1
ISBN 1-59084-559-5 (series)

Design by Lori Holland.
Composition by Bytheway Publishing Services, Binghamton, New York.
Cover design by Benjamin Stewart.
Printed and bound in the Hashemite Kingdom of Jordan.

This book is meant to educate and should not be used as an alternative to appropriate medical care. Its creators have made every effort to ensure that the information presented is accurate— but it is not intended to substitute for the help and services of trained professionals.

Picture Credits:
Artville: pp. 36, 48, 58, 59, 76, 80, 86, 100, 105, 106, 122. Autumn Libal: pp. 12, 16, 20, 23, 27, 33, 40, 53, 61, 62, 68, 75, 85, 90, 96, 109, 114, 117, 120, 121. Comstock: pp. 50, 56. Corbis: pp. 30, 89. Corel: pp. 42, 45, 66, 70. National Library of Medicine: pp. 37, 39. Metatools: p. 34. PhotoDisc: pp. 46, 54, 73, 112. Rubberball: pp. 10, 82. Stockbyte: pp. 41, 64, 79, 102. The individuals in these images are models, and the images are for illustrative purposes only.

CONTENTS

INTRODUCTION

by Mary Ann Johnson

Teenagers have reason to be interested in psychiatric disorders and their treatment. Friends, family members, and even teens themselves may experience one of these disorders. Using scenarios adolescents will understand, this series explains various psychiatric disorders and the drugs that treat them.

Diagnosis and treatment of psychiatric disorders in children between six and eighteen years old are well studied and documented in the scientific journals. In 1998, Roberts and colleagues identified and reviewed fifty-two research studies that attempted to identify the overall prevalence of child and adolescent psychiatric disorders. Estimates of prevalence in this review ranged from one percent to nearly 51 percent. Various other studies have reported similar findings. Needless to say, many children and adolescents are suffering from psychiatric disorders and are in need of treatment.

Many children have more than one psychiatric disorder, which complicates their diagnoses and treatment plans. Psychiatric disorders often occur together. For instance, a person with a sleep disorder may also be depressed; a teenager with attention-deficit/hyperactivity disorder (ADHD) may also have a substance-use disorder. In psychiatry, we call this comorbidity. Much research addressing this issue has led to improved diagnosis and treatment.

The most common child and adolescent psychiatric disorders are anxiety disorders, depressive disorders, and ADHD. Sleep disorders, sexual disorders, eating disorders, substance-abuse disorders, and psychotic disorders are also quite common. This series has volumes that address each of these disorders.

Major depressive disorders have been the most commonly diagnosed mood disorders for children and adolescents. Researchers don't agree as to how common mania and bipolar disorder are in children. Some experts believe that manic episodes in children and adolescents are underdiagnosed. Many times, a mood disturbance may co-occur with another psychiatric disorder. For instance, children with ADHD may also be depressed. ADHD is just one psychiatric disorder that is a major health concern for children, adolescents, and adults. Studies of ADHD have reported prevalence rates among children that range from two to 12 percent.

Failure to understand or seek treatment for psychiatric disorders puts children and young adults at risk of developing substance-use disorders. For example, recent research indicates that those with ADHD who were treated with medication were 85 percent less likely to develop a substance-use disorder. Results like these emphasize the importance of timely diagnosis and treatment.

Early diagnosis and treatment may prevent these children from developing further psychological problems. Books like those in this series provide important information, a vital first step toward increased awareness of psychological disorders; knowledge and understanding can shed light on even the most difficult subject. These books should never, however, be viewed as a substitute for professional consultation. Psychiatric testing and an evaluation by a licensed professional are recommended to determine the needs of the child or adolescent and to establish an appropriate treatment plan.

FOREWORD

by Donald Esherick

We live in a society filled with technology—from computers surfing the Internet to automobiles operating on gas and batteries. In the midst of this advanced society, diseases, illnesses, and medical conditions are treated and often cured with the administration of drugs, many of which were unknown thirty years ago. In the United States, we are fortunate to have an agency, the Food and Drug Administration (FDA), which monitors the development of new drugs and then determines whether the new drugs are safe and effective for use in human beings.

When a new drug is developed, a pharmaceutical company usually intends that drug to treat a single disease or family of diseases. The FDA reviews the company's research to determine if the drug is safe for use in the population at large and if it effectively treats the targeted illnesses. When the FDA finds that the drug is safe and effective, it approves the drug for treating that specific disease or condition. This is called the labeled indication.

During the routine use of the drug, the pharmaceutical company and physicians often observe that a drug treats other medical conditions besides what is indicated in the labeling. While the labeling will not include the treatment of the particular condition, a physician can still prescribe the drug to a patient with this disease. This is known as an unlabeled or off-label indication. This series contains information about both the labeled and off-label indications of psychiatric drugs.

I have reviewed the books in this series from the perspective of the pharmaceutical industry and the FDA, specifically focusing on the labeled indications, uses, and known side effects of these drugs. Further information can be found on the FDA's Web page (www.FDA.gov).

Everyone daydreams sometimes—but people with dissociative disorders may become totally disconnected from the reality around them.

1 | What Are Dissociative Disorders?

Ruth is a good student and likes school, but so far her Monday hasn't been going well at all. It started at breakfast. Ruth's mom was talking, and Ruth was playing with her oatmeal. She scooped the creamy glop up and watched it dribble off her spoon. Resting her head on her hand, Ruth gave a deep sigh and stared at her breakfast bowl as though she were hypnotized.

"Ruth!" Her mother's voice startled her. "Did you hear anything I said?"

Ruth looked up. Her mother's eyebrows pulled tight together as the school bus honked outside. Ruth rolled her eyes. "Yes," she replied in an exasperated tone. She hurriedly stuffed her unfinished homework into her backpack.

"So you'll have all that done when I get home?"

"Yeeessss!" Ruth said again, even more exasperated. But as she stepped onto the bus, fear flip-flopped in her stomach. What had her mom been talking about? Ruth didn't know.

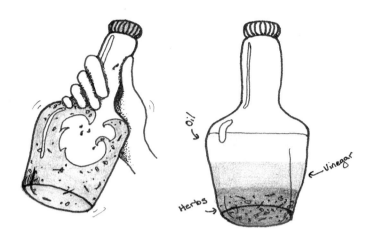

*When you shake a bottle of salad dressing, the ingredients be-
come "integrated"—but when you set the bottle down, the oil,
vinegar, and herbs become "dissociated."*

In her first class things didn't go much better. She stared
out the window while the teacher took attendance. "Jake,"
the teacher called out. Ruth noticed two birds in the bush
outside. "Peter," the teacher droned on. Ruth felt the warmth
of the bright sun flowing through the glass. "Ruth." It
seemed far too nice a day to be sitting indoors, Ruth thought.

"Ruth."

And what was it that her mother had been talking about
anyway, she wondered.

"Ruth!"

Someone kicked the back of Ruth's chair, and she sat up
with a start. "Here!" Ruth yelped and slumped into her chair,
her face red.

Things only got worse as the day rolled on. Ruth was late
getting to her third class. At lunch she realized she'd forgotten to bring in her overdue library books. At the end of her fi-

nal class, Ruth was shocked to find the teacher already collecting the test papers. Ruth looked down at her own test to see that she had spaced out after the third question! Not believing how her day had gone, Ruth flopped her head down on the desk. "What's wrong with me?" she moaned.

DISCUSSION

In the above story, Ruth is experiencing something known as dissociation. To *dissociate* means to remove or separate from something. For example, when you shake a bottle of salad dressing, the contents mix together, or **integrate**, with one another. However, when you set the bottle down, the oil rises to the top and the vinegar sinks to the bottom. The ingredients of the salad dressing have become dissociated from one another.

> **GLOSSARY**
>
> *integrate*: To combine separate parts into a whole.

In our typical daily functioning we are integrated with our world. We feel, observe, smell, touch, remember, and think about the things around us. When experiencing a dissociative state, however, we separate from part or all of our immediate surroundings. For example, have you ever daydreamed, lost track of time when you were having fun, or "tuned out" when your parents were scolding you? If so, you were experiencing dissociation.

When Ruth dissociates at school, she asks if something is "wrong" with her. Though it may feel as if something is not right, there is nothing all that unusual about Ruth's situation. Routine dissociation is something that we all encounter in our daily activities. Ruth is simply having what we all have sometimes, a bad day.

Some people, however, enter dissociative states that are much more severe than what Ruth is experiencing. These dissociative states can lead to memory lapses, anxiety, and

GLOSSARY

trauma: *From a psychological view, an event that can cause extreme emotional reaction.*

amnesia: *A loss of memory due to injury, fatigue, traumatic, or stressful event. It can be a symptom of a psychological or physical disorder.*

fugue: *In the psychiatric sense, an amnesia state in which one is or appears to be aware of one's actions, but cannot remember them on returning to a normal state.*

difficulty working and interacting with people. When dissociation becomes this severe, it may be part of what is known as a dissociative disorder.

Dissociative disorders are psychological disorders. While physical disorders are illnesses of the body, psychological disorders are illnesses of the mind. Our minds are responsible for our emotions, the development of our personalities, learning, and many other important functions. In most people, all of these mental processes work together, allowing the person to experience, function in, and adapt to her changing world. When a person has a dissociative disorder, these mental processes no longer work together. Some mental processes, like memory, may separate from the other processes, such as behavior and personality. The person may be unable to think clearly in a situation that requires focused concentration—like a job interview—or be unable to access their emotions in a situation that requires emotional expression—like a loving relationship.

Severe stress or *trauma*, such as that caused by childhood abuse or battlefield experiences in war, are the causes of dissociative disorders. These situations, or things that threaten to remind the person of the trauma, can trigger dissociative states. There are four main types of dissociative disorders: dissociative *amnesia*, dissociative *fugue*, dissociative identity disorder (once called multiple personality disorder), and depersonalization disorder.

DISSOCIATIVE AMNESIA

This dissociative disorder makes a person unable to remember important parts of her life. If the person was abused as a child, she may not be able to remember much of her childhood because her mind is dissociating, or "hiding," the memories. Uncomfortable, traumatic, or stressful events may trigger a person with dissociative amnesia to also forget things that happen in the present. This is the mind's way of trying to protect the person from the painful memories of the past.

DISSOCIATIVE FUGUE

The main symptom of dissociative fugue is when a person unexpectedly travels or "runs away" from his home, work, or established life. Like dissociative amnesia, the person cannot remember important information from his past, but threatening or stressful situations cause the person to not only *mentally* dissociate from the situation but also to *physically* dissociate by going to a new location. This travel may be brief; for example, the person may "wake up" to find himself a few miles from home with no recollection of traveling there. However, these fugue states can also last for extended periods of time. In this case, the person might even move to a different city and assume a new identity. Months later he could return to his pre-fugue state with no idea where he is, what he has been doing, or how long he has been gone.

DISSOCIATIVE IDENTITY DISORDER

This was once called multiple personality disorder. In dissociative identity disorder (DID), a person's identity is fractured into two or more distinct personality states. The different personalities control the person's behavior at different times and may be completely unaware of the other personalities' existence. A person with DID may seem to be completely different people at different times. However, one

must remember that a person with DID is not a collection of different people who are sharing the same body. Rather, a person with DID is one person who experiences herself as having separate parts of her mind (sometimes felt as separate personalities) that work independently of each other. The switching of personality states causes the person with DID to have many of the same symptoms of dissociative amnesia and dissociative fugue.

DEPERSONALIZATION DISORDER

With this dissociative disorder the person feels detached or separated from her mind or body. Unlike dissociative amne-

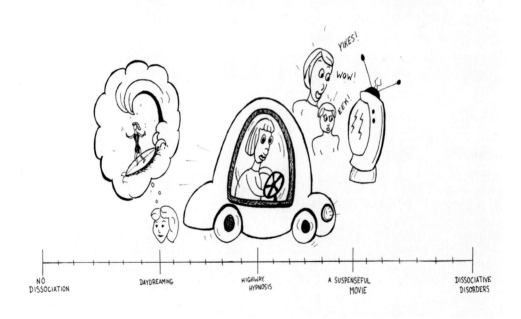

Feelings of dissociation exist across a range of possible responses; a dissociative disorder is at the extreme end of this range.

Our minds have many aspects. We have internal mental processes like thoughts, emotions, and memories. We also have external mental processes like speech and behavior. Our minds work hard to keep our thoughts, emotions, and behavior in the appropriate balance for the specific situation. For example, in class, one's "thinking" mind takes control while the person's emotions are distant. When talking with a loved one, the person's emotions may come forward while the person's "thinking" mind becomes less active. Sometimes one mental function may take too much control, causing the person to act inappropriately. For example, in an argument with a friend, feelings of sadness and anger may overpower one's rational thinking and cause the person to say something hurtful or untrue.

sia, dissociative fugue, and DID, the person with depersonalization disorder may have all her memories intact and yet feel separate from them, as if the things she remembers did not actually happen to her. A person with depersonalization disorder may describe herself as feeling as though she is watching someone else. She may also have physical sensations of detachment such as numbness or an inability to feel pain.

GLOSSARY

neurological: *Of or relating to the nervous system.*

Dissociative symptoms can occur for many reasons, but not every person with severe dissociation has a dissociative disorder. Some people experience dissociation in response to drugs, **neurological** disorders, or other medical conditions. Such symptoms are not dissociative disorders because they have physical rather than psychological causes. However, some people suffer from serious dissociative symptoms that are psychologically based but do not meet the criteria for one of the specific disorders mentioned above. Such a person may be said to have a "dissociative disorder not otherwise specified." This means that the person's dissociative symptoms are disabling enough to be considered a disorder but do not fit the definition of any particular disorder.

Below are some more examples of people experiencing dissociation. As you read, ask yourself these questions:

1. Can you relate to the person's experience?
2. Do you think the person's experience might suggest a disorder?
3. Do you think the symptoms are part of a dissociative disorder or a different medical condition? Why?
4. What would you do if you had this experience?

GLOSSARY

powwow circuit: Traveling exhibition of Native American dance, music, and culture.

EXAMPLE 1

Joel had been traveling the ***powwow circuit*** with his family for as long as he could remember: New Mexico, Tennessee, New York, Massachusetts, Ontario, British Columbia, South Dakota, and so many other places. His family circled the continent year after year. Joel and his cousins were dancers. His father played the drum, and his uncles sang the traditional songs of their people.

From the time that he could walk, Joel loved to dance with his cousins. He loved to hear the men's voices rising together like a great bird spreading its wings over everything. He loved the way the drum made his feet vibrate, then tap, then dance. But as a little boy, though he loved to dance, Joel hadn't liked dancing in the powwows.

When it was time to dance at the powwows, people gathered in a great circle. Hundreds of people. Joel would look at their faces. People were smiling, laughing, and talking. Some people watched curiously while others waited anxiously for the dances to begin. The drum would start beating out its solid rhythm, and he felt like all the people's eyes were on him. The singers' voices would rise up, and the circle of dancers would begin to move. But all Joel could think about were the people watching him. Instead of hearing the drum, he heard people whispering and someone's baby crying. Sweat began to trickle down his side, and his heart beat faster. He would try to concentrate on the drum but he would stumble, and the bells around his ankles clanged out of rhythm with the other dancers. When he and his cousins danced alone, Joel felt great joy and freedom. But dancing in front of the audience made him feel panicked and anxious. He began to dread the dances. Finally, he told his father about how he felt.

"It sounds like you're suffering from stage fright, Joel," his father said to him smiling.

"I just feel like they're all staring at me. I trip and make mistakes. I feel like they're laughing at me," Joel confided. "I love to dance, but they make me afraid. When they are there, I don't know if I want to dance."

"I understand," his father said with a sympathetic look. "Maybe you need to ask yourself why you think dancing is important. When I play the drum I do not think about the audience. I think about my father, who taught me to play, and his father who taught him. When I play the drum my brothers start singing, and I feel like we are all together again, like when our father was alive. I do not play for the people watching, but I am happy that they are there so that they can learn about our family and our traditions. The next time you dance close your eyes, pretend that the people aren't there, and listen to the drum and your cousins dancing around you. See what happens."

Joel thought his father's suggestion seemed like good advice. At the next powwow, when the dancing circle formed, he closed his eyes and took a deep breath. As the drum began, he tried to block out everything from his mind except the sound of the drum. He felt the rhythm of the drum in his feet and creeping up his legs. He heard the sound of the bells jingling as his feet began to move up and down. Then his un-

Our internal thoughts and memories, as well as our external behaviors and speech, shape the people we are.

cles' voices began to fill his brain. He concentrated on their voices as they rose and fell like waves lapping at the shore, rolling from great peaks to quiet valleys of sound. The sounds filled his mind, growing larger as he began to dance faster and faster with the beating of the drum. The sound of his blood pulsing in his ears joined with the music of the voices and the drum. He felt his body expanding out, becoming part of the swishing grass and jangling bells, part of his uncles' voices and his father's drum. Then he felt himself grow bigger, so big that there was no time or space. He felt the old and new mix together into one great presence. His grandfather and his grandfather's father, and all that they had seen and known, were right there in the moving of Joel's feet and the beating of the drum. He danced and danced, but did not know how long. When the drum finally stopped, he opened his eyes. There were smiling faces all around him. People were clapping, and for a moment Joel was surprised because he had forgotten that they were there at all.

Discussion

In this example we see a common type of dissociation. Joel dissociates himself from the people around him so that he can overcome his stage fright. Unlike dissociation caused by trauma, intentional dissociation can be a useful and beneficial part of life. For example, in Lamaze classes, women learn to dissociate themselves from the pain of childbirth so they can give birth without medication. Doctors sometimes suggest methods of intentional dissociation, like yoga, meditation, and hypnosis, to help patients relieve stress and live healthier lives. Many cultures and religions use these and other types of dissociation as part of worship and spiritual experiences. These types of dissociation should not be considered abnormal or part of a disorder, and doctors should be aware of patients' cultural and religious backgrounds when discussing dissociative disorders.

EXAMPLE 2

Sandra was lying on her bed in her sunny, brightly painted room. A book was open on her lap, but she was having trouble focusing. She would stop reading for minutes at a time. Sometimes she would repeat the same word fifteen times before moving on to the next word. The book began to slip from her grasp. It slipped, slowly at first, across her hand and to the edge of the bed where gravity caught it and pulled it to the floor. Sandra's head snapped back against the wall. Her eyes rolled back and her hands began to twitch.

Three hours later Sandra opened her eyes. Everything appeared small and distant. The walls and furniture had fuzzy edges, as if everything was out of focus. Her father sat on a chair with his head craning toward her. His body looked far away, and he seemed to be reaching forward from somewhere deep in a long gray tunnel. His mouth opened and closed, but Sandra heard no sound. Her grandmother and brother were standing by her father's chair. Everyone moved slowly, as if they had been caught in a bottle of molasses. Sandra tried to speak, but her family didn't seem to notice. She dragged her mind from their faces and concentrated on moving her lips. Her tongue flopped and rolled around the words, "I . . . m . . . must . . . have . . . fall . . . en . . . a . . . sleep." It came out like one long and oozing word.

"Sandra." Her father's voice sounded like it was coming from under water. "Sandra, you had a *seizure*."

"I . . . did?" She couldn't seem to get her mouth to work right.

"Did you take your medicine this morning?" Her grandmother's words pushed through the long dark tunnel to Sandra's ears. She tried to think, but a thick fog blanketed the words. She tried to concentrate on what her grandmother asked, but it was like the words were swirling in a dark whirlpool just out of her reach.

"Sandra," her grandmother tried again. "Did you take your *epilepsy* medicine this morning?"

Sandra blinked at each word and carefully repeated the question in her mind. Medicine, her grandmother was asking about medicine. This morning . . . what happened this morning? She was confused. What did she do this morning? What time was it now? Why was everything moving so slowly? She opened her mouth to speak again.

"I . . . can't . . . re . . . mem . . . ber."

GLOSSARY

seizure: A physical reaction sometimes caused by brain injury or high fever.

epilepsy: A physical disorder that can be caused by many things, including brain injury. Symptoms can include seizures or memory loss.

A person with a dissociative disorder may feel as though he is looking at reality from far away. This experience may be confusing and frightening.

Discussion

Like Ruth and Joel, Sandra is experiencing a dissociative state. Her mind is separated from the world around her, making her confused. Things seem to be moving slowly, and objects look far away and out of focus. She doesn't know what happened to her, and she can't remember what she did that day. Unlike Ruth and Joel, however, Sandra's dissociation is not an average or harmless experience. Her dissociation is part of a physical medical condition.

Sandra's dissociation is caused by epileptic seizures. The increased brain activity that causes Sandra to have a seizure also affects her awareness and perception. Many people who have seizures and other types of medical conditions experience dissociative states as symptoms of their condition. However, such people are not suffering from a dissociative disorder. If a person's dissociative states, like Sandra's, have physical, neurological, or chemical causes, then they are not dissociative disorders.

EXAMPLE 3

Kyle twirled dizzily in the dark. He raised the broom handle and lunged forward with all his strength. Thwack! Everyone squealed. The sun streaked his eyes as he tore the blindfold off. The ring of children collapsed upon him. Kyle looked up. The piñata spun crazily on its yellow string, a hole broken into its colorful side. He watched as its candy insides rained down on the children's heads; he'd never had so much fun.

Kyle joined the other laughing six-year-olds searching for the glossy wrappers sprinkled across the carpet of grass. It was Julie's birthday party. Julie was Kyle's best friend, and she was old. She was turning seven. He couldn't wait to be big like Julie, but his birthday wasn't for six more months, and that was a long ways away.

"Cake time kids!" a parent called. The child-sized mob rushed for the picnic table and jostled for seats. The sliding door to the house squeaked open, and Julie's mother stepped out carrying a white cake. The icing swirled like snowdrifts around the sides, and pink-frosting roses smiled over the edge of the plate. Atop the cake, seven candles blazed.

"Ready everyone?" Julie's mom hummed. "Happy birth-day to you." Julie's mom placed the cake upon the table. Julie kneeled on her chair for a better look and clapped happily.

"Happy birthday, dear Julie." Kyle turned with a smile toward his friend, but something caught his eye. The can-dles. He stared into their bright light.

"Happy birthday to you. . ." The song spun away. From far away he heard everyone clap.

Julie took a big breath and held it. She leaned over and blew as hard as she could. Whoosh! The candles went out, leaving little blue smoke trails in their wake. A huge smile spread across Julie's face. Kyle felt a strange sense of relief and clapped with the other children. But then the quiet little candletips began to glow, and one by one their small flames sprang back to life. A hush fell over the children as they looked suspiciously at the white-icing cake. The parents ex-changed knowing smiles.

"Go ahead, Julie. Try again. They're tricky." Julie's mom winked across the table at Kyle's mom. As Kyle looked at the cake, his stomach gave a little turn. Julie's chest heaved and she blew again. Again the candles went out . . . but a second later their flames popped right back up. A few parents laughed.

"What am I doing wrong, Mom?" Julie asked.

"Oh, nothing, honey. Maybe your friends need to help. Everyone get close to the cake. On the count of three, we'll all blow the candles out." The children leaned toward the cake. No one noticed that Kyle had slumped down in his chair.

Kyle watched the other children lean close to the can-dles. "One. . ." They all took a deep breath. "Two. . ." They craned toward the little flames.

"It's okay. It just got wet. We'll get a new cake."

Kyle looked relieved. "I'm tired, Mom." His eyelids began to droop and close. His mom scooped him up and went inside to lay him down. Julie's mom raced in after her, closing the glass door behind her. The children and guests began to whisper in the yard.

The two women took Kyle to Julie's bedroom and laid him down. Kyle's mother turned.

"I am so sorry about this. It just never occurred to me that the candles would be a problem."

"What happened?" Julie's mother asked, fear in her voice. "Is he going to be all right?"

"He'll be okay. It's the strangest thing. Lately he has these . . . episodes. We think it's from this." She rolled up her shirtsleeve. Her arm was purple with scars. Julie's mother gasped.

"He was so little. He could barely talk," Kyle's mother continued. "His father and I were roasting marshmallows in the backyard. Kyle was playing in the grass. I reached over to poke the logs, and when I looked down, my shirt was on fire. It went up so fast, for a second we were just staring at it, like we were frozen. Then Kyle began to scream, and it was like we all jolted awake. Kyle's father grabbed the picnic blanket and threw it over me. It really wasn't that bad."

Julie's mother looked stricken. "No, really," Kyle's mother said. "My arm is scarred, but we were lucky. It could have been so much worse. My arm got better and everything was fine, until lately. I never really thought about it anymore, and Kyle says he doesn't remember. But these past few weeks he's suddenly begun having these. . ." She paused and gestured with her hand. "These *flashbacks* or something. I don't know what to do. I'm so sorry about your party."

"Don't be ridiculous," Julie's mother said, taking Kyle's mother's arm. "I just want to make sure Kyle's all right. It

GLOSSARY

flashbacks: The reliving of a past, often traumatic, incident.

doesn't seem like such a big deal to you now, but for such a small child, that event, seeing his mother on fire, must have been horribly traumatic. Maybe you should take him to a doctor, just to see what the doctor says."

Kyle's mom let out an exhausted sigh. "Maybe you're right. We should see a doctor. I think we need to help Kyle before this gets any worse."

Discussion

In this final example, we see behavior that may be part of a dissociative disorder. Unlike the other examples of dissociation, Kyle's experience cannot be explained by the normal ways that we experience dissociation in our everyday lives or by a medical condition. Like Kyle, some people with dissociative disorders experience "flashbacks." In these flashbacks, they relive the traumatic experience. When the person "wakes up," however, he has no memory of the flashback or the event he was reliving. When symptoms like these interfere with a person's everyday life and functioning, a consultation with a trained professional—like a doctor, psychologist, or counselor—should be considered.

When a person has a dissociative disorder, psychiatric drugs may be used to treat some of the accompanying symptoms.

2 | The History of Therapy and Drug Treatment

Janet couldn't remember the last time she felt "normal." In fact, she could hardly remember anything. Her brain felt foggy and numb. Sometimes she imagined herself kneeling on a great frozen lake. She pressed her face against the ice, trying to see through the thick cloudy surface to the open water below. She knew it must be freezing, but her body didn't feel cold. In fact, she didn't feel any physical sensation at all, just an internal panic. She didn't understand these feelings or the image of herself on the ice. She just knew that she was lost above the ice and that the knowledge that could save her was trapped in the dark, unreachable water below.

When she first spoke to a psychiatrist about these feelings he asked her about her health, her life, her family, and her emotions. She tried to describe her feelings of loss and hopelessness. She said she felt trapped, unable to move. She said she had no energy, felt like she couldn't face getting out of bed, and was suspicious and frightened around other peo-

GLOSSARY

antidepressant: Medication prescribed to help people suffering from extreme sadness.

clinical depression: A state of sadness that is longstanding and pervades the person's entire life.

ple. Her psychiatrist thought that an ***antidepressant*** might help. Janet thought so, too, so she began taking medication.

Janet's doctor explained to her that he thought she might be suffering from ***clinical depression*** caused by a chemical imbalance in her brain. He explained that although the medication could help restore the chemical balance and allow her to feel more in control of her emotions, it could not simply make her happy. Janet would still have to work hard—not only by taking her medication regularly but also by doing things like eating right, exercising, setting a healthy sleep schedule, and engaging in social activities. Furthermore, the doctor warned, the medication might take a few weeks to fully establish any positive effects. Janet would have to be patient.

Janet did everything the doctor prescribed. She took her medication every day and began an exercise program. She tried to eat right, went to bed at ten o'clock every evening, and woke up at seven o'clock every morning. She even invited people from school over for a party and attended a high school dance. But she could tell it wasn't helping. The harder she tried, the more frustrated she got. She found herself talk-

In some serious dissociative disorders, a person's symptoms may be so overwhelming that it is difficult to treat the underlying condition. If true healing is to begin, however, it is imperative that patients be properly diagnosed and treated. Think about what would happen if you broke a bone in your leg. Your leg would hurt, swell, and have lots of bruising. Now imagine that you go to the doctor, and the doctor prescribes a powerful painkiller and sends you home. For a little while, your leg might feel better, but it is still broken. The doctor has only treated your symptom, not your actual ailment, and the next time you try to walk you will realize that your problem is just as bad as it was before receiving treatment.

Janet told her psychiatrist that "Sara" was trapped beneath the ice.

ing constantly, even though no one was around but herself. Her days began to fill with dark spots of time that she could not remember. She felt more and more disconnected. She began to miss school and lose sleep. She'd find notes that she'd written to herself but couldn't remember writing. They said things like "Janet! Help Me!" and "Who are you?" Scariest of all, she began hearing voices in her head that did not sound like her own. When she imagined herself looking down through that barren ice, she thought she saw a little girl looking back at her. She was sure the little girl's name was Sara.

The next time Janet saw her psychiatrist, she told him that Sara was trapped beneath the ice. Her psychiatrist looked puzzled and asked Janet to explain what she meant. Janet told her psychiatrist about the voices and her strange memory losses. He asked if anyone in her family had ***schizophrenia***. The doctor asked if these voices ever told her to harm herself. She said that sometimes they did but that she

GLOSSARY

schizophrenia: A psychiatric disorder characterized by a loss of contact with reality. Symptoms can include auditory and visual hallucinations.

Multiple personalities is one form of dissociative disorder. Each personality may handle a different part of the individual's emotional life.

knew these voices came from within her. She tried to explain that she knew there weren't people outside of her talking to her. She said it felt almost like *she* was saying these things, but as different people . . . as if she were different people. The doctor listened with concern. He explained to Janet that what she was describing sounded like **psychotic** symptoms. He suggested that Janet begin taking lithium in addition to her antidepressants.

DISCUSSION

Although she and her doctor do not know it, Janet is suffering from dissociative identity disorder, or DID for short. As a child, Janet suffered severe physical and emotional abuse, so horrible that her mind blocked it from her memory. Even though Janet is not consciously aware of these memories, they are still present in her mind where they are causing great pain and confusion, leading to a dissociative disorder.

Janet is experiencing a common problem in the diagnosis and treatment of dissociative disorders. Her doctor has prescribed medications for depression and schizophrenia, yet Janet is not getting better. Unfortunately, dissociative disorders have a long history of **misdiagnosis**, improper medication, and false hope. There is no medication approved for the treatment of dissociative disorders, and there is no research or systematic study of medication as a major possibility for treatment. Nevertheless, most patients with dissociative disorders have received, and continue to receive, medication in the course of their treatment. A significant number of these patients have, like Janet, been prescribed medication because of a misdiagnosis.

Historically, the treatment of dissociative disorders has been filled with fear, suspicion, and doubt. People with disorders like DID were sometimes thought to be possessed and

GLOSSARY

exorcisms: Religious ceremonies to rid a person from Satan or other satanic forces.

electroshock therapies: Treatments for psychiatric disorders, especially depression, through the use of an electric current passed into the brain.

borderline personality disorder: A serious mental illness where a person demonstrates instability in moods, interpersonal relationships, self-image, and behavior. This instability often disrupts family and work life, long-term planning, and the individual's sense of identity.

treated with **exorcisms**. Others endured experimental **electroshock therapies**, while others were told they were making their symptoms up as an excuse for inappropriate, unhealthy, or violent behavior. Even today, despite numerous diagnoses and detailed accounts of patients' experiences, there are still those in the medical field who debate the existence of these disorders, especially DID. Even among those well educated in the field, misdiagnosis remains a major problem in the treatment of dissociative disorders.

Dissociative disorders are sometimes difficult to identify because their symptoms occur in many other types of illnesses. People with conditions like schizophrenia, **borderline personality disorder**, and **bipolar disorder** often experience the same symptoms that individuals with dissociative disorders experience. When a person with dissociative symptoms first seeks treatment, it may be difficult for the doctor to discover whether the person is suffering from a dissocia-

A person with a dissociative disorder often feels disconnected from pieces of himself!

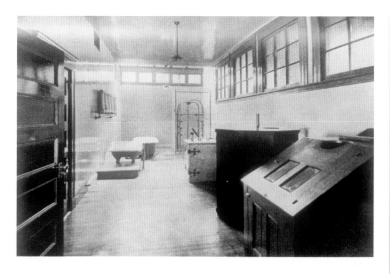

In the past, people with dissociative disorders were often misdiagnosed and shut away in psychiatric asylums like this one.

tive disorder or from dissociative symptoms resulting from a different type of disorder—physical or psychological.

This problem is not unique to dissociative disorders. Many medical conditions share common symptoms. For example, many different things can cause chest pain, including a pulled muscle, heartburn, a fractured rib, or a heart attack. In order to treat the chest pain, the doctor must first determine what type of illness is causing the chest pain. A person with chest pain may think that he is having heartburn when he is really having a heart attack. Even though both conditions cause chest pain, treating the person for heartburn will not solve the problem of his heart attack. A similar thing can happen to patients with dissociative disorders. Perhaps one of the dissociative patient's symptoms is fatigue. Many things, including clinical depression, *anemia*, and DID, can cause fatigue. If the patient's fatigue is

paranoid delusions: Unfounded feelings of being persecuted or belief that one has excessive value.

auditory hallucination: Something that one hears but that is not really there.

caused by DID, giving her a medication for anemia will not improve her condition.

DID is commonly misdiagnosed because so many of its symptoms can be mistaken for schizophrenia and other psychotic disorders. A major reason for this misdiagnosis is that the patient may, like Janet, speak of hearing voices. A person with schizophrenia or *paranoid delusions* may hear voices, believe people are watching them, or feel constantly threatened and pursued. A person talking about symptoms of a dissociative disorder may describe similar things.

The major distinguishing factor between dissociative disorders and schizophrenia and other psychoses is that the person with a dissociative disorder generally does not lose touch with reality. Although she may hear voices, she knows that the voices are coming from within herself and may even be surprised to know that other people don't hear voices in their heads. People with schizophrenia and other psychotic disorders tend to lose touch with reality, often believing in things that are not there. The voices they hear may be *auditory hallucinations* that seem to actually be outside themselves. The voices that a person with DID hears are interior voices communicating inside the person's mind.

Using the example of a broken bone again, imagine that your broken bone punctured an artery. The doctor cannot set the bone because the punctured artery is a more immediate threat to your health and life. The doctor must first stop the bleeding, reduce swelling, and stabilize your condition. Once he has done all that, he can begin to fix the original source of the problem—the broken bone. When used effectively, psychiatric drugs play a similar role in the treatment of dissociative disorders. They can be used to "stop the bleeding" of the overly traumatized mind. When the patient is stabilized, the true treatment can begin.

In ages past, the voices some people heard inside their heads were blamed on demons.

GLOSSARY

compartmentalize: To separate into different parts or categories.

ego: The conscious self or sense of self that controls thought and behavior. The ego is aware of and feels separate from the external world.

alter: In the psychiatric sense, an alternative ego or personality state who periodically takes control of the body.

Unlike psychotic disorders, the cause of dissociative disorders can be traced back to past events to which the mind and body are still reacting. When severe trauma occurs with which a person cannot cope, the brain might **compartmentalize** it, or "package it up," to hide the event from the person's memories and consciousness. The person does not *want* to remember, perhaps *can't bear* to remember, so the brain hides the event from the memory. The person forgets it ever happened.

When someone suffers, as Janet does, from such severe and repeated abuse that DID results, her brain has gone one step beyond hiding the memory to creating another personality, an alternative **ego** or **alter**, to deal with the abuse. The alternative ego state may have many of the qualities of an independent person, even its own name.

When something bad happens, the human brain may package up the memories and negative emotions and keep them hidden from the conscious mind.

Dissociation is one way children cope with abuse.

Janet was severely abused as a child and created an alternative personality in her mind to deal with the abuse. This alternative personality's name is Sara. Sara is seven years old, the age Janet was during the most severe abuse. Whenever the abuse began, Janet "disappeared" into her mind and "Sara" came out. In effect, this allowed Janet's conscious mind to believe: "I'm not abused. Sara is." Over time, Sara became an established part of Janet's functioning. Janet lost all conscious awareness of Sara's existence. She lost her memory of the things that happened to her when she was being Sara.

Now that Janet is older, she hears voices. The voices belong to Sara and the other alternative egos Janet created to deal with her abuse, but Janet does not know who Sara is or why she's there. Janet can't control Sara the way she could when she was a child. Janet may find it difficult to accept

Veterans of the Vietnam War experienced many psychological scars, including dissociative symptoms.

that Sara is really a part of herself and that the things that happened to Sara were really things that happened to her.

It is easy to see why a person who is unfamiliar with dissociative disorders may think that Janet has schizophrenia or a psychotic disorder. What has really happened, however, is that Janet entered into an incredibly complex system of forgetting that was necessary for her to survive her abuse. Her experiences were too terrible to simply forget, so Janet's brain created Sara in an attempt to deal with the past while still protecting Janet emotionally from the painful abuse.

Historically, a number of different attitudes have influenced the recognition and treatment of dissociative patients. In the nineteenth century, individuals at the forefront of psychiatry recognized dissociation as a part of human behavior. In the early-twentieth century, however, Freud and like-minded thinkers in the field of psychiatry rejected the belief in dissociation as a mode of human behavior, thereby eliminating the possibility that psychiatric disorders could be based on dissociative mental functioning. Patients with high levels of dissociation were sometimes labeled as *hysterical* and treated with drastic measures such as electroshock therapy. (Electroshock therapy does sometimes help individuals with extremely severe seizures and some other disorders, but the medical field has learned that it is not an appropriate treatment for dissociative disorders.) During this same time period, schizophrenia was recognized and defined as a mental disorder. Many dissociative patients were given this diagnosis and labeled psychotic by the medical field.

In the late 1970s, however, things began to change again. Thousands of soldiers returned from Vietnam, many of them bearing overwhelming psychological scars from the trauma they experienced there. Soldiers suffered from memory lapses, fugue states, flashbacks, and other dissociative and post-traumatic stress related symptoms. The field of psychiatry began to reevaluate its attitude toward trauma and its

GLOSSARY

hysterical: Having physical, mental, and emotional ailments and abnormalities that have no physical cause.

effects on the mind and body. Psychiatrists saw that many soldiers could not leave the horrors of war on the battlefield, but continued to carry the pain and torture in their minds even years after the traumatic events occurred. Some psychiatrists found that therapy, even when it was as simple as providing a safe place where a soldier could talk about what happened to him, helped people to grieve, accept, and recover from their battlefield experiences.

In this time period, the women's movement was also giving voice to many societal issues that had previously remained buried. One of the issues that this movement helped bring to the public's attention was the issue of childhood

---

The Food and Drug Administration (FDA) is the U.S. agency that determines whether a drug is safe or not; no drug can be sold in the United States without the FDA's approval.

Not all FDA-approved drugs are approved for people of all ages. In other words, the FDA can approve a drug for use in adults, but not for use in children or teens. Because child, adolescent, and adult physiologies vary, drugs can impact their bodies differently. What is safe for an adult's body could be dangerous for a teen or a child. The FDA will approve a drug for use only in the patient group the drug safely treats. When a drug is approved for adults, but not children or teens, it means the drug is safe for adults, but it may pose dangers for non-adults. In some cases, the FDA cannot approve a drug's usage for teens or children simply because the drug was tested only on adults; the FDA cannot predict how adolescents and children might respond to the medication. Some doctors may feel the drug is safe for teens—but the FDA does not have the research to back its official approval.

Until recent years, few studies were done on medications for children and adolescents with psychiatric disorders. As a result, most psychiatric drugs are not FDA-approved for children and adolescents, and "off-label" use is standard in pediatric psychopharmacology.

Victims of abuse may continue to reexperience traumatic events years later.

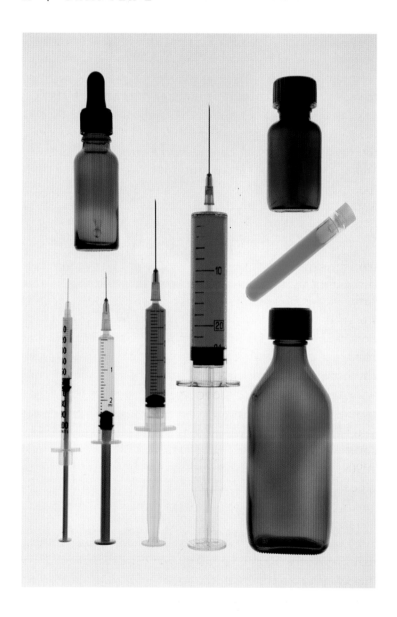

There are no medications that are specifically intended to treat dissociative disorders—but practitioners may prescribe psychiatric drugs to ease the anxiety or depression that often accompanies a dissociative disorder.

physical and sexual abuse. Modern medicine and the general public began to realize that abuse of children was far more common than previously thought and that trauma could have much more devastating and longer lasting effects than anyone had previously believed. Changing attitudes led to the recognition of a new category of mental illness, dissociative disorders, defined for the first time in the *Diagnostic and Statistical Manual*, Third Edition (DSM-III). At this time, therapists began using different forms of psychoanalysis, or "talk therapy," including hypnosis, to uncover the memories that seemed to be at the root of patients' dissociation.

Throughout the 1970s and 1980s, even the popular media had an effect on attitudes toward dissociative illnesses. Books like *Sybil* and *The Three Faces of Eve* (first published earlier in 1957) became popular. They told heart-wrenching stories of childhood abuse and struggles with DID. The images of DID, or multiple personalities, portrayed in popular culture in the 1980s contributed to a backlash against psychotherapy and dissociative disorders themselves. People accused therapists of using hypnosis to create false memories in their patients, making their patients believe in things that had never happened and leading their patients into discoveries of abuse that never occurred. In the 1980s and 1990s, psychiatrists also learned that uncovering too many hidden memories or uncovering painful memories too quickly can harm the patient even more by causing them to be retraumatized.

Today, much has been learned about psychodynamic therapy in the treatment of dissociative disorders. Most therapists know that it is important to establish a trusting professional relationship with their patient and that uncovering past memories should be done carefully and only to the extent that it can help the patient. Therapists who treat patients with dissociative disorders should also be careful when using hypnosis because people with dissociative disor-

Therapy should help a person with a dissociative disorder find her way back to reality.

ders are much more easily hypnotized than most members of the population. Hypnosis therefore should always be carefully monitored and controlled.

Although there are no medications that specifically treat dissociative disorders, many psychiatrists find medications helpful during certain stages of treatment. For example, a person with a severe dissociative disorder may become so filled with anxiety, frustration, depression, and confusion that she becomes suicidal. In such instances, psychotherapy cannot begin until the patient is stabilized and out of danger of harming herself or others. Psychiatric drugs such as antidepressants, antianxiety drugs, and antipsychotics may be used to stabilize the patient.

If a psychiatrist decides that medication might help a patient with a dissociative disorder, the psychiatrist must be very careful to look at the patient *holistically*. Different personality states may have different symptoms and complaints. Taking numerous medications for different symptoms is unnecessary and can be harmful. The psychiatrist should try to determine the underlying problem behind the symptoms and then decide which symptoms, if any, can be alleviated with medication.

GLOSSARY

holistically: Seeing the interdependence of separate parts, focusing on the whole rather than on pieces of the whole.

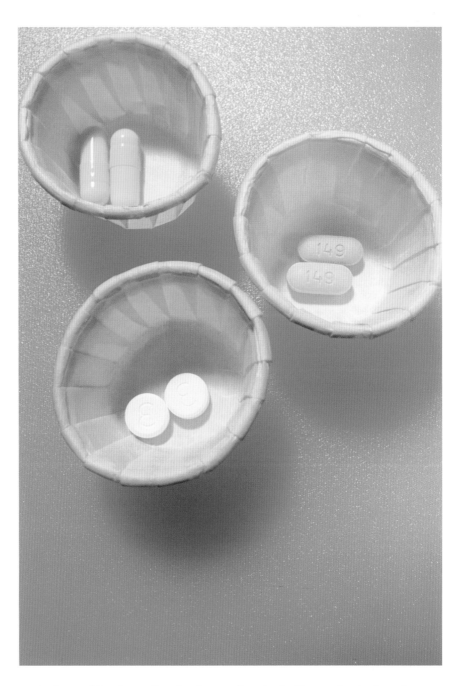

Each psychiatric medication has a chemical effect on brain function.

3 | How Some Drugs Work

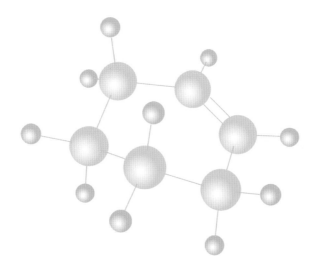

When Lisette woke up in the hospital, she had no idea where she was. Two police officers stood at the foot of her bed. She lifted her head to look at them, but a searing pain ran through her neck and down her spine. She gasped.

"No, don't get up, Lisette," the female officer said, reaching toward her. "Just try to relax. We're here to help you."

Her head throbbed. She squinted against the bright lights of the white hospital room and blinked hard. Her eyes searched the room for clues. She could see her hands propped up on pillows on each side of her body. Deep red slashes crisscrossed over angry purple bruises on her up-turned palms. Her whole body ached, and her tongue felt swollen and dry. "What happened to me?" she whispered to the woman in uniform beside her.

"Well, that's what we're here to find out." The male officer stepped forward. "We got the call last night. You stumbled into the emergency room. The doctors and nurses didn't see anyone with you. Can you remember how you got here?"

Lisette thought hard. Last night? What had happened last night? She had no memory of coming to the hospital. "No." She hesitated. "I don't know how I got here." She could feel panic rising from somewhere deep inside of her. Taking two deep breaths, she tried to push the panic down. It was like fighting against a rising tide.

"What's the last thing you remember, Lisette?" the female officer prodded gently.

Lisette's thoughts felt muddy, as if quicksand had filled her mind. She fought to maintain control. "I came home from work. I was going to eat dinner, but my dog wanted to go out. I decided to take him for a walk. Usually we walk to this coffeehouse five blocks up, but I decided to take him to the park instead." She stopped, because she couldn't breathe. She felt like she was choking.

"And then what happened?" the other officer encouraged.

Lisette paused a moment. "That's it," she finally said. "That's all I remember, walking out the door and turning toward the park." Then a terrible thought occurred to her. "Boomer!" she yelled at the police officers. They jumped, startled. "Boomer, my dog," she cried desperately. "Where is he? Is he okay?" The panic had broken over the dam and spilled through her body and mind. She suddenly knew that something terrible had happened to her, even though she did not know what it was. She was crying, gasping for breath. She tried to get up, tearing at the tubes in her arms. The female officer reached for her, attempting to calm her.

"Lisette, it's okay. We'll check all the animal shelters for your dog. Take deep breaths. It's okay. We're going to help you." The officer stepped to the hallway and called for a nurse. "Keep breathing, Lisette. We're going to have the

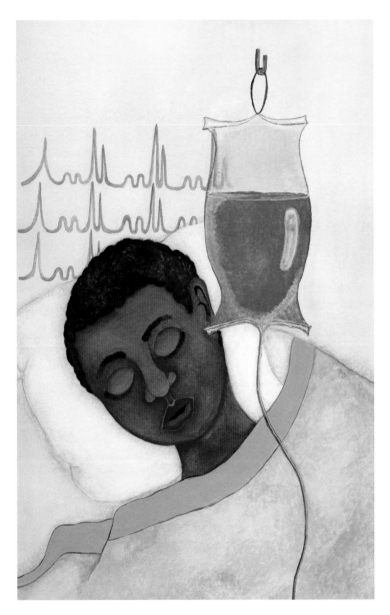

A person with a dissociative disorder may need to be hospitalized if her symptoms are severe enough.

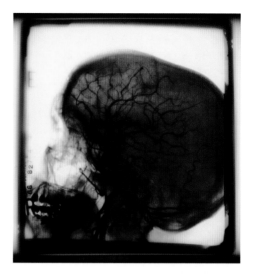

The mind and body work together, which means that psychological conditions can have physical symptoms.

nurse come and give you some Valium. That should help you relax. We can talk later, when you feel a little more calm."

DISCUSSION

Many in the scientific community now believe that trauma can affect brain chemistry. No one, however, is quite sure how. Nevertheless, this may be the reason why so many people with dissociative disorders also suffer from coexisting disorders like depression, **anxiety**, and eating disorders. Even though the dissociative disorders themselves are psychological disorders, these coexisting disorders sometimes have chemical or physical causes. The mind and body work together in complicated ways, and psychological conditions can produce physical changes that warrant medicinal treat-

GLOSSARY

anxiety: Psychiatrically, an overwhelming sense of fear, often characterized by sweating, rapid pulse, and tension.

ment. In the above story, Lisette is experiencing dissociative amnesia after a traumatic event. Her inability to recall the traumatic event is a psychological reaction. The panic she feels, however, is a physical reaction. The police officers hope that calming her physically with medication will make dealing with her psychological pain more manageable.

There is a great range of symptoms experienced by dissociative patients, and a great range of psychiatric medications may be prescribed. Because there are no drugs that treat dissociative disorders directly, it is impossible to speak of any specific drug and its treatment of dissociative disorders. Rather, because of the great range of symptoms experienced by people with dissociative disorders, any psychiatric drug might be employed for use, depending on the particulars of the case. For example, one patient with a dissociative disorder may be prescribed a psychiatric drug for depression, while another patient is temporarily prescribed a drug to help her sleep, and yet another patient receives no drug treatment at all. There are more than one hundred psychotherapeutic agents listed in the *Physicians' Desk Reference*. Out of the numerous psychiatric drugs on the market, including antidepressants, antianxiety agents, and antipsychotic drugs, the particular one to be prescribed would be chosen at the discretion of the medical caregiver.

Although none of the psychiatric drugs available treat dissociative disorders, the nature of dissociative disorders should still be considered carefully when prescribing such drugs to dissociative patients for coexisting conditions. For example, it is common for a person with a dissociative disorder to suffer from depressive symptoms, so a

> The fact that antidepressants are usually combined with therapy creates some debate in measuring antidepressants' effectiveness as a supplementary treatment to dissociative disorders. If, after some weeks the patient's mood improves, it may be difficult, or even impossible, to determine whether the improvement is due to the medication, progress in therapy, or a combination of the two.

When taking a psychiatric medication, it is important to follow the pharmacist's and prescribing practitioner's instructions.

psychiatrist may wish to prescribe an antidepressant. However, it is also common for people with dissociative disorders to have a very high level of daily anxiety. The clinician needs to assess symptoms and risk factors carefully to choose the right medication for each person with a dissociative disorder.

Antidepressants work by adjusting the balance of chemicals in a person's brain. However, the chemical balance in our bodies is constantly changing in response to numerous environmental, physical, and emotional factors. You will

Brand Names vs. Generic Names

Talking about psychiatric drugs can be confusing, because every drug has at least two names: its "generic name" and the "brand name" that the pharmaceutical company uses to market the drug. Generic names come from the drugs' chemical structures, while drug companies use brand names to inspire public recognition and loyalty for their products.

Here are the brand names and generic names for some common psychiatric drugs:

Celexa®	citalopram
Haldol®	haloperidol
Luvox®	fluvoxamine
Paxil®	paroxetine hydrochloride
Prozac®	fluoxetine hydrochloride
Risperdal®	risperidone
Zoloft®	sertraline hydrochloride

We all have many different emotions during the course of any given day.

feel many different sensations and emotions during the course of the day: you may be angry one moment, frightened the next, and laughing just a little while later. You may feel tired for an hour, and then have a surge of energy. These ups and downs are normal and necessary. Antidepressants do not give a person "happy" chemicals, thereby removing all the downs the person might feel. Rather, antidepressants work to bring the body's own chemicals into a healthy balance so that the person's daily experiences of highs and lows are more moderate. It takes time for this balance to be achieved, and it is usually a number of weeks before an antidepressant medication has a significant affect on a person's depressive mood. In the case of dissociative disorders, the patient should be undergoing psychodynamic therapy at the same time.

Psychiatric drugs help a person achieve emotional and chemical balance.

There are a variety of benzodiazepines, each sold under a different trade name.

Drug	Trade Name
alprazolam	Xanax
chlordiazepoxide	Librium
clonazepam	Klonopin
clorazepate	Tranxene
dazepam	Valium
lorazepam	Ativan

Selective serotonin reuptake inhibitors (SSRIs) are the most commonly prescribed antidepressants. Having too little serotonin in our bodies can affect our moods, sleep, eating habits, learning, and many other important functions. In some people, the cells that produce serotonin begin to reabsorb the serotonin before it can go out and perform its job in the body. SSRIs, like Prozac, Paxil, Zoloft, Celexa, and Luvox, keep the cells from reabsorbing the serotonin. Preventing reabsorption allows the serotonin to stay in the body longer, hopefully leading to an increase in serotonin levels and an improvement in the patient's quality of life. The SSRIs are often a good choice for patients with dissociative disorders because these antidepressants have a low incidence of side effects. They are the first line of treatment for both depressive and anxiety disorders.

A class of psychiatric drugs known as benzodiazepines, like Ativan, Xanax, Klonopin, and Valium, might be prescribed to a patient for anxiety. Unlike antidepressants, benzodiazepines work quickly to produce a calming effect, so

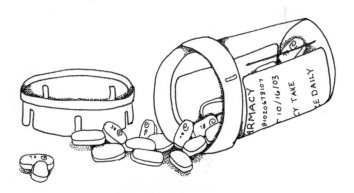

Medication may help a person with a dissociative disorder think more clearly so that she can take better advantage of other forms of therapy.

they can be useful in helping a person in an immediate crisis situation. Lisette, for example, is in a moment of crisis. Her trauma has just occurred, and she will need time to rest and recover before she can think more clearly. Taking Valium for a brief amount of time may help stabilize her condition so that she can begin to discover what happened to her. How-

Adrenaline is the same hormone that floods the bodies of wild animals when they are under attack. This hormone gives them a sudden burst of strength, which can mean the difference between life and death. If adrenaline levels in a person stay high, however, the person will have difficulty functioning in normal situations because the brain has turned off thinking and the body has turned on to fight or run.

ever, because benzodiazepines act so quickly, they can also be very addictive. They need to be used carefully and usually are prescribed only as a temporary measure until an SSRI can take effect.

Like benzodiazepines, beta-blockers are also used in treating anxiety. They block adrenaline, which the body naturally produces in response to anxiety-provoking situations. The release of adrenaline causes the heart rate to rise, muscles to be flooded with blood and oxygen, and energy to surge. If a person is in danger, this flood of energy is vital so the person can protect himself or escape.

A beta-blocker can help a person experiencing things like traumatic flashbacks by blocking the adrenaline that is part of the body's immediate fight-or-flight response. In some people, the temporary blocking of emotional and physical responses to past trauma can create precious openings for therapy to begin.

Dopamine-blocking drugs, like Haldol and Risperdal, are sometimes (though rarely) prescribed for people with dissociative disorders. This may happens because the person has been misdiagnosed as having schizophrenia or some other psychotic disorder. At other times, the person may be properly diagnosed as having a dissociative disorder and given a dopamine-blocking drug in the hopes of reducing flashbacks and other dissociative symptoms. It is important to remember that these antipsychotic drugs affect different people's brains in very different ways. In people with psychotic disorders, these drugs can usually be tolerated in large amounts and help to regulate the person's symptoms so she can lead a more normal life. In people without psychotic disorders, however, very low doses of antipsychotics tend to have a highly *sedative* affect. Dissociative disorders are *not* psychotic disorders. When antipsychotic drugs are helpful, it is usually because they stabilize moods and cause sedation, thereby lessening the disturbing flashbacks and dissociative

GLOSSARY

sedative: Something with a calming or soothing effect.

Adrenalin stimulates the "fight-or-flight" response to anxiety-provoking situations.

A person with a dissociative disorder may repress disturbing events and yet still experience flashbacks that can be as frightening as the original event was.

symptoms. This relief of symptoms through sedation can be very helpful in extreme crisis situations (like admittance to a psychiatric hospital for a suicide attempt). They should in no way, however, be considered a long-term solution to dissociation that is caused by the effects and reliving of unresolved trauma.

Soldiers in the armed forces may encounter disturbing events that will follow them the rest of their lives.

4 | Treatment Description

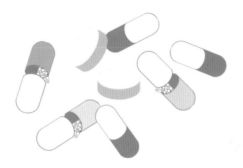

Jerry was only seventeen years old when he was sent to Vietnam. Four of his friends had enlisted the day before. At school they talked about how they were going to serve their country. His friends told him that they were going to go fight for freedom. Their words sounded important and noble. They talked about it as if it would be a great adventure, and they made Vietnam sound like it was a tropical paradise with lush jungles fading into sandy beaches. They said that they would return as heroes.

It all sounded pretty good. Their talk made Jerry wonder what he was doing with his life, so after school he went and signed up. That night his mother cried and cried. Now, five years later, he knew why she had cried.

His stay in Vietnam was nothing like his friends said it would be. The jungles were wet, steaming, and crawling with biting insects. Every footstep forward felt like it would be his last. He thought he had known fear before, but now he knew terror. Night after night passed sleepless. Every sound threatened disaster. Every birdcall raised suspicion. Every snapping twig brought visions of enemy guns.

Then, one day it happened. He and six other soldiers stepped out of the jungle and into a village. Everything was silent, abandoned looking, but unnaturally still. Everyone stopped, afraid to move, afraid to breathe. Then, out of nowhere, a small hard object sailed toward them.

That was all he remembered.

When he first returned home—one arm in a sling, one leg gone—he was so drugged up on painkillers that he couldn't tell what was real. Sometimes he would look around at the clean, white sheets, the softly scented flowers, and think that he must have died back there in Vietnam. But then at night he was all too sure that he was alive, alive back in Vietnam, in that village, living a horrible nightmare.

Dreams of past events may seem like reality to a person suffering from a dissociative disorder.

One morning his mother came into his room. Through the fog he saw that she had a black eye. He asked what had happened. All she would say was that he had a nightmare, and she had tried to wake him up. Apparently, he had slugged her.

The doctors assured his family that once he was off the painkillers these troubling symptoms would go away. They were wrong. For five years the symptoms had continued. Sometimes he'd feel completely fine and then a car would backfire, and an hour later he would "wake up" crouching under the kitchen table. He crawled out of bed in the mornings feeling like he hadn't slept at all. His parents looked like they hadn't slept either. He'd ask what was wrong, and they would tell him that he had screamed all night long. He did not remember screaming. He began to think that he was losing his mind . . . or maybe he'd lost it already. Maybe it had been sucked down into the jungle mud with his blood in Vietnam.

Finally, he decided to see a psychiatrist. He told her of his memory lapses and nightmares. She asked him to tell her about Vietnam. He said he could not remember, and she suggested they try hypnosis to retrieve the locked away memories.

Jerry began to describe the scene to his psychiatrist: They stepped out of the jungle and into the deathly quiet village. Everyone stopped. He held his breath. He watched as a small hard object sailed toward them.

"Grenade!" the soldier beside him screamed, and the whole place erupted. He fired his gun; he didn't know at whom. Bullets sprayed back at him, but he didn't know from where. Suddenly people were running from the huts, unarmed people screaming and waving their hands. Soldiers were behind them, weapons vomiting out volley after volley. And he and his comrades just kept firing, at everything. Bullets tore into the unarmed people and the soldiers alike.

A soldier's bravery and dedication during times of war cannot save him from psychological problems down the road.

Then a bullet tore into him. The first one hit his leg, shattering his knee. The second tore through his shoulder and he fell to the ground. He watched, horrified, as his own red blood mixed with the brown mud. A long plaintive shriek pierced his ears and mind. A little girl fell on top of him, blank dead eyes staring into his own. He opened his mouth and heard his own scream mix with the echoes of the girl's last cry.

"Jerry," a gentle voice called. "Jerry, open your eyes."

He opened his eyes. He was in an office. He was on the floor. Tears were streaming down his face. His head felt like it was exploding. All the horrible memories were there. The girl's eyes, he could see her eyes staring through him.

"Jerry, you are not in Vietnam," she said. "You are in my office. You are twenty-two years old." He blinked at the girl. No, she wasn't the girl. She was a grown woman, a doctor. She was his psychiatrist. He was in his psychiatrist's office.

"That must have been terrible for you, Jerry," she said. "But I want you to know that you are safe. None of those things can touch you now. They are memories. They are not really happening."

"But it feels like it's happening. It feels like it's happening right now," he moaned. "They were hostages. They thought we were coming to save them, but we killed them. I killed her," he sobbed. The anguish rose up in his throat to choke him.

"Jerry, it's not your fault," the psychiatrist spoke again. "You could not have known. Many terrible things happened, but they weren't your fault. We will work together to get through this. But first, I need you to find a place where you can go when the memories threaten to overwhelm you. It needs to be a safe place, a room in your mind that is filled with comforting things. It is a secret room. Only you know where it is. It has a lock on the door so nothing bad can get in. Whenever you feel yourself being overwhelmed and slip-

Medications Used to Treat Depression

Selective serotonin reuptake inhibitors (SSRIs)
Tricyclic antidepressants (TCAs)
Monoamine oxidase inhibitors (MAOIs)
Heterocyclic antidepressants
Miscellaneous drugs like Wellbutrin, Ludiomil, Remeron, and Effexor

GLOSSARY

spontaneous:
Unplanned.

ping into the past, I want you to go to this room where nothing bad can touch you."

DISCUSSION

Contrary to popular belief, dissociative disorders can be cured. Many psychiatric disorders such as depression, anxiety disorders, and schizophrenia can be treated with medication—but not cured. Once properly diagnosed and treated by a knowledgeable therapist, dissociative disorders do have a high rate of cure. Nevertheless, to achieve improvement, most patients must engage in a long and often traumatic journey of discovery.

Jerry is suffering from dissociative amnesia caused by the trauma he experienced in Vietnam. Through intensive psychotherapy, patients with dissociative amnesia and other dissociative disorders work to discover forgotten memories of trauma or abuse that the brain is trying to hide. For some people with dissociative amnesia caused by an individual event, like a bad car accident, simply uncovering the memory can lead to a *spontaneous* cure of the dissociative amnesia. For others, especially for those whose trauma occurred over an extended period of time, discovering the hidden memories and making peace with the trauma of the past is just the starting point of therapy.

Psychotherapy is a very individual treatment, and each person's treatment plan will be different. Nevertheless, there are some helpful guidelines that many therapists recommend when beginning a treatment program. The first and most important step in therapy is to establish a secure environment for the patient where he can feel protected from the

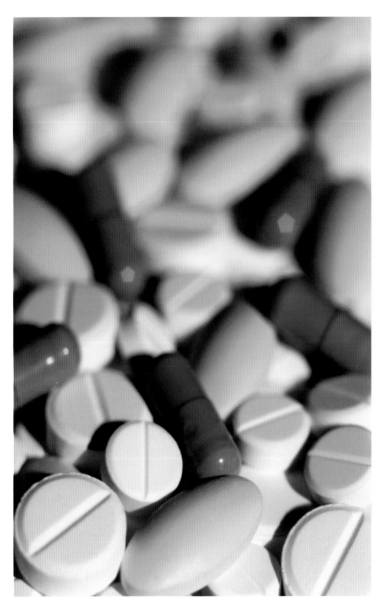

There are a number of medications used to treat depression.

> ## "Off-Label" Treatment
>
> The FDA bases its approval on specific research results. Sometimes, a particular use for a drug may have been thoroughly researched by many studies, while other uses lack the same amount of research. In that case, the drug label will only include the uses that have met the FDA's stringent research requirements. Physicians, however, may continue to prescribe that drug for other "off-label" uses. For instance, according to the labels found on beta-blockers, these medicines are approved for treating high blood pressure; medical practitioners, however, commonly prescribe beta-blockers for psychiatric uses.

stress that is causing the dissociative states. The patient should feel both physically and emotionally safe. The therapist's office should be a place of trust and security. Many therapists also help their patients to create a safe place in their minds. This is usually a room that the patient can imagine going to when he feels threatened. In Jerry's case, the room will be a place where he can escape from the traumatic flashbacks he has of Vietnam. The patient fills the room with comforting objects and soothing imagery. Therapists might instruct the patient to imagine a strong lock on the door of the room so that he can keep bad thoughts or painful emotions from entering the room.

Once a safe place has been established where therapy can take place, the doctor and patient should discuss the goals of therapy. Over the course of treatment, patients and therapists should periodically review the theraputic goals. Checking in on goals can help patients determine if they are making progress. Additionally, the goals one begins with when starting therapy may change over time. One might realize that a specific goal is unreasonable for her time frame. On the other hand, one might find that she surpassed a goal long ago and that it is time to set new goals. For people with dissociative disorders, therapy can be a process with both ups and downs. Expectations for therapy should be reasonable and flexible. Patients should understand that needing to alter goals or slow the pace of therapy is in no way a failure; it is simply an adjustment for their current needs.

Recovery of the patient's personal identity is often the first goal of treatment for those with dissociative disorders. Identifying and reintegrating repressed memories into the

Psychotherapy should provide a person with a "safe place."

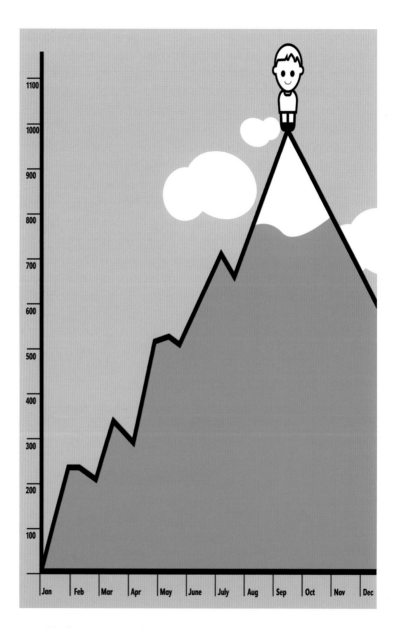

Establishing and defining goals is an important part of good therapy.

The major goal of therapy for patients with DID is usually to achieve integration of the different alters into the person's one main personality, or to get all the different alters to be aware of and cooperate with each other to lead as normal a life as possible. When beginning the communication process between alters, therapists often recommend that the patient get a journal where all the different personalities can express themselves. People with DID often find that a journal is a place where the different parts of themselves can talk to each other. Each personality has an opportunity to control the pen and then read what everyone else wrote.

patient's personal history is another important goal. Patients with DID make working toward integration of personality, or cooperation between states, an important priority. The most central goal of therapy is usually returning the patient to her previous life or equipping her with the necessary skills for building a healthier life.

Defining and developing boundaries is another important step in beginning the treatment process. Many therapists believe that there should be no physical contact between the doctor and the patient. Respecting physical barriers can be especially important for patients with dissociative disorders because so many of them suffered abuse at the hands of people they trusted. Setting clear guidelines at the beginning of therapy regarding physical contact can help make the therapist's office a safe space.

Treatment scheduling can also have an important impact on a patient's progress. A patient who has dissociative amnesia caused by a single traumatic event may only need a few appointments before he is able to continue the healing process without a therapist's aid. Other patients may need more time. Jerry, for example, is struggling not only with the

trauma from the battlefield but also with his guilt about the situation. Complicated situations like Jerry's often require longer treatment.

Patients with dissociative identity disorder will need to spend much more time in therapy than will most patients with other dissociative disorders. DID patients usually faced **recurrent** trauma and abuse over long periods of time. For them, dissociation has become a way of life. Dissociation may be the only way they know for coping not just with trauma but with any uncomfortable or difficult situation. Once they have discovered the hidden traumas that caused them to begin to dissociate, they must learn to stop dissociating. This means learning to confront problems and uncomfortable situations instead of running away from them. Many patients with DID must relearn how to interact with others and learn, perhaps for the first time, how to trust other people.

Because of their traumatic histories, many people's intensive psychotherapy can be a long and painful process with many setbacks. Psychotherapeutic treatment for DID usually lasts three to five years, or longer. Even with the long treatment program, however, dissociative disorders as severe as DID do have very positive **prognoses** for improvement and cure. Unfortunately, there are many examples of people spending as many as twenty years misdiagnosed and improperly medicated before finding proper diagnosis and treatment.

Most therapists recommend that DID patients have two therapy sessions per week. Therapy sessions are usually one hour to one and a half hours long. Patients who have just been diagnosed or who are facing serious crises may require more time per week. Giving a patient too much time, however, can have adverse affects. A patient can begin to rely too much on her therapist or begin to doubt her ability to function without the therapist's aid. There are many different

A person with a dissociative disorder may feel as though the frightened child she once was still lives inside her.

types of therapists who might treat a patient with a dissociative disorder. Patients may attend therapy sessions with psychologists, psychiatrists, social workers, or school crisis counselors, or may participate in self-help groups. Only psychiatrists, psychiatric clinical nurse specialists, nurse practitioners, or medical doctors, however, may prescribe medication. If a therapist like a psychologist or school counselor thinks medication could be a helpful supplement to therapy, she must refer her patient to a psychiatrist or other psychiatric practitioner for a consultation.

The different psychiatric drugs that may be used to supplement psychotherapy are most helpful in specific stages of treatment. Benzodiazepines, some antipsychotic medications, and sleep aids are most helpful in the early stages of diagnosis and treatment if the patient's condition needs to be stabilized. For some people, stabilization may take a few days; for others it takes weeks or even months. Furthermore,

To some extent, all of us carry our younger selves inside us; but a person with a dissociative disorder is unable to interact completely with today's reality because of past pain.

a patient may stabilize only to relapse when he encounters difficulties in therapy. Some people find that once stabilized, medication is no longer a necessary or appropriate part of treatment.

Once the hard work of long-term treatment has begun, different types of medication are more appropriate. During the course of psychotherapy, the patient works to uncover the hidden pain and trauma that is causing him to dissociate. For some people, however, discovering the truth hidden in the past can cause a whole new devastation. Working through these memories can sometimes lead to slipping further into depression while trying to come to terms with the past. During this long and difficult stage of therapy, antidepressants such as Prozac or another SSRI and mood stabilizers like Depakote, and Lithium are usually more appropriate than benzodiazepines and other drugs used in the initial stages of treatment.

Whereas some people find that once the source of their disorder is treated, they are able to proceed without medication, others may find that trauma has an irreversible effect on their mind and body. The dissociative disorder may be cured, but a coexisting depressive disorder might make medication a necessary part of the rest of a patient's life. The medical practitioner will periodically reevaluate patients to see if their medication can be tapered off. Patients should never stop taking a medication without consulting first with their practitioner.

Many people, not just those with psychiatric conditions, live and thrive because of the help of medication. People with conditions like severe asthma and diabetes must always take medication to maintain good health. Long-term medication for depression and other psychiatric conditions can be thought of in the same way.

When a child experiences something extremely difficult, it may lead to a dissociative disorder—but this does not mean that he is "crazy."

5 | Case Studies

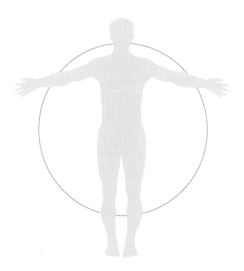

People with dissociative disorders are not weird or "nuts." They are real-life people, people like you or your friends, who have experienced something very difficult in their lives. Their disorder is the way they have coped with that trauma. The following case studies may help you understand a bit better the nature of these disorders.

A CASE STUDY IN DISSOCIATIVE AMNESIA

Nathan was ten years old when the Mississippi River flooded. The whole world watched images on the news of people stacking sandbags and the muddy water rising. Nathan, however, hadn't watched the rising water on the news; he watched it in his house. For days his family had eyed the water creeping steadily up their yard. They had joined those sandbag armies constructing makeshift dams, trying to keep the water at bay. They thought they would still have time to leave the house if it became necessary, but when the water suddenly broke through the manmade barriers, it rose in minutes. His father had grabbed him while his mother reached for his little sister. They crawled through an upstairs window out onto their porch roof. They huddled together in the rain, watching the water rise all around them. Four hours later a helicopter rescued them. On the news that night the whole world watched as their house floated away.

At first Nathan's parents thought it was a blessing that he didn't remember anything from that day. But soon after, he began having nightmares. He slept less and less. Eventually he could only fall asleep lying between his parents in their bed. He then began having trouble while awake: He started staring off into space, staying mute for hours at a time. He refused to take baths or showers and would only wash with a washcloth. His parents tried to talk to him about the flood, but he said he didn't know what they were talking about. He said he didn't remember anything like that ever happening. They asked him what he was thinking about when he stared into space, but he said he didn't know. His parents began to lose patience, thinking that he simply needed to stop behaving this way. One day his mother told him that he couldn't come out of the bathroom until he had taken a shower. Hours passed, and the bathroom was silent. She started to regret being so harsh, but she didn't know what else to do. Finally, she opened the bathroom door. Nathan was curled up, sleeping in the bathtub. His arms were locked tightly around his head in a protective ball. She shook him gently. When he looked up at her with his tear-stained face, she too started to cry.

Nathan's parents realized that he was suffering from something more serious than simple misbehavior. When they took him to see a child psychologist, she explained how

Nathan's experience in the flood eventually made him afraid of water, even when it was as harmless as a shower or a bath.

Those with a dissociative disorder keep their traumatic memories carefully locked away inside their minds.

trauma can affect the mind. She told them that she thought Nathan was trying to block out the memories of the flood but that they haunted him anyway. She called his condition dissociative amnesia and said that the best way to treat it would be to get Nathan to remember what had happened. Nathan's parents were resistant to the idea at first. If the memories were causing this much pain for him while they were hidden, wouldn't they cause even more pain when they were out in the open? The psychologist explained that this usually wasn't the case. She said that Nathan had an internal conflict. Part of him was denying that anything bad had ever happened. At the same time, another part of him kept insisting that something terrible had occurred. She described these conflicting feelings as creating a war inside of him. She said that the first step to healing is acceptance and that as long as Nathan denied what had happened to him, he wouldn't be able to heal and move past it.

Nathan and the psychologist worked together for a number of weeks establishing a trusting relationship. For their first few sessions, they didn't talk very much about Nathan's nightmares and blackouts. Instead, they talked about his favorite foods, the games he liked, how he was getting along with his little sister, and all kinds of other regular things. After four therapy sessions, Nathan began talking about his nightmares on his own. His therapist felt that this was the sign she needed. Once he was ready to bring up these difficult topics, they were ready to take the therapy to the next level. Over the next few weeks, they talked about the flood and the things that Nathan did and did not remember. The final breakthrough in his therapy happened one day when the psychologist brought in a videotape. She asked Nathan's whole family to come to the session. His parents explained to him that they were going to watch a tape of what really happened that day. They put their arms around him and asked if he was ready. He said he was.

The tape the psychiatrist played was the newscast of the house being carried away by the floodwaters. The psychiatrist asked Nathan if he knew what was happening. He looked wide-eyed at the screen. Suddenly his face filled with fear and wonder. It was *their* house, he told them. He said he remembered that day. They had been wet and cold on the roof with water rising all around them. Then a helicopter had come and lifted them away. He had looked out the window and saw the house swallowed up below.

After recovering his memories, Nathan's nightmares stopped almost immediately. His therapist warned, however, that this did not mean that all of his feelings toward the event had been resolved. He continued to see his therapist once a week for the following year. He stopped blacking out and no longer feared water. By the end of his therapy, he still felt sad and frightened whenever he thought about the flood. His therapist explained that those feelings were natural and

Nathan's psychologist used video images to trigger Nathan's memory. Living with a dissociative disorder is very hard, and many dissociative patients go through periods of extreme denial. It is impossible for a person to improve or cure her disorder if she denies that the disorder exists. Because people with dissociative amnesia and other dissociative disorders often do not remember their dissociative behavior, it is easy for them to slip into denial. Therapists will sometimes tape a session with a dissociative patient and then play the tape back for the patient. Seeing herself dissociating on tape is something a patient cannot usually deny, and this technique has helped many people overcome their denial. Taping and replaying a patient's session should, of course, always be done with the patient's full knowledge and approval.

appropriate emotions. His dissociative amnesia had been cured—and no psychiatric drugs had been needed.

A CASE STUDY IN DISSOCIATIVE FUGUE

Joan had been so excited about becoming a mother. It was all she ever wanted. But when she looked at that little baby lying in her arms, completely dependent on her for strength and happiness, her heart filled with fear. She was determined to give her daughter a wonderful life, but she had no idea how to achieve that. When she walked away from the hospital holding a new little life in her arms, she started to fear the worst.

As Joan began taking care of her new baby, she started to panic about everything. Every night she checked and rechecked to make sure her daughter was breathing. She was afraid of everything. She was afraid the baby would get sick and afraid the baby would get too hungry. She stopped letting other people hold the baby because she was afraid they would drop her. But then Joan started fearing that she herself would drop her. She would hesitate at the side of the crib, afraid to go near her daughter, afraid of hurting her. One night, Joan "woke up" to find herself standing in the street wearing only her nightgown. She could hear her daughter screaming in the house and raced inside. The baby was lying in her crib, crying but safe. Joan, however, was shaken to her core. What had she been doing in the street? Why hadn't she been with her baby? What could have happened while she was out of the house?

Joan knew that she needed professional help. She began seeing a psychiatrist who diagnosed her with ***postpartum*** depression. He said that some mothers suffer from this condition after giving birth and that antidepressants can help. Joan took the medication, faithfully following her doctor's every order. He had told her that it might take some time to

> **GLOSSARY**
>
> ***postpartum***: The period following giving birth.

After a woman goes through childbirth, the hormonal changes in her body may cause depression.

Most women who experience postpartum depression do not also experience dissociative symptoms—but Joan's experiences made her vulnerable to past pain at a time of new stress.

begin feeling better, but months went by and nothing changed. In fact, her symptoms got worse. She started leaving the house without realizing it. One time she even found herself in a parking lot miles from home. She had no idea how she had gotten there or where her daughter was. She was so afraid to be alone with her daughter and of putting her daughter in danger that she hired a live-in nanny.

Joan begged her psychiatrist for help. She told him she must be suffering from something other than postpartum depression and he agreed. He said that her traveling sounded like fugue states, in which she was trying to dissociate herself from something threatening or painful.

In the following therapy sessions the psychiatrist began exploring Joan's life history, asking her detailed questions about her own childhood and relationship with her mother. Joan realized that she had very few memories from before the age of ten. Joan's mother died when Joan was twelve. When Joan tried to remember her past, she felt like there was a dark hole where memories of her mother should have been. Joan's psychiatrist decided to try hypnosis to discover what Joan was blocking from her memory.

The following weeks were perhaps the most painful weeks in Joan's life. She uncovered memories that she had thought were buried forever. When Joan was a child her mother had abused her. The years of abuse were again vivid in Joan's mind. The memories seemed unbearable at times, but Joan also began to remember how, growing up, she had been determined to someday be a wonderful mother—the type of mother she had never had. She began to understand that her treatment toward her daughter was based on fear. Although she wanted to be a loving mother, part of her was afraid of hurting her daughter the same way her mother had hurt her. She feared being a bad mother so much that she was trying to run away from being a mother at all.

Every inch of the paper was covered with writing. Some of the writing was scrawled in frantic scribbles. Some sentences were printed with large, wavering letters. Others rolled across the paper in perfectly sweeping cursive. The writing looked like a conversation between three different people.

"Did you write this?" Stanley squirmed in his seat and nodded his head.

"All of it?" she asked. He shook his head, squirming even more. Dr. O'Donnel was shocked by how childlike Stanley suddenly looked. She turned the paper over. On the back was a child's drawing of a little boy. Tears dropped from the little boy's eyes. The words "Hurt Danny" were printed in large letters next to the picture. Suddenly, Dr. O'Donnel thought she might know from what Stanley was suffering. "Which part of this did you write?" she asked him. Without meeting her gaze, he pointed at the drawing.

"Do you know who wrote the other parts?" There was a long pause.

"No, b-b-but Stanley does," he stuttered.

Dr. O'Donnel sat back in surprise. "What is your name?" she asked gently.

"D-d-d-danny."

Dr. O'Donnel took a deep breath. "And how old are you, Danny?"

Stanley looked at his hands and counted on his fingers. He held four fingers up in the air for Dr. O'Donnel to see. "I'm four."

Dr. O'Donnel realized that Stanley was suffering from DID and that his strange behavior was caused by the separate personalities within him, all trying to come forward and have a voice. Once Stanley was properly diagnosed, the therapy sessions improved dramatically. Dr. O'Donnel asked Stanley to begin keeping a journal. She told him to dedicate at least one hour every day to writing in the journal. She taught him to relax and allow the different personalities to come out so that they could each take a turn writing in the journal. The journal became a valuable tool for discovering what types of conflicts were going on in the different parts of Stanley's mind.

But proper diagnosis brought its own problems for Stanley. He found that there was a great *stigma* attached to having DID. For two years he fluctuated between denial and acceptance. At times he hated himself and all the warring personalities inside of him.

Therapy was often difficult, too. Dr. O'Donnel helped Stanley look into his past to try to discover what caused his dissociative disorder. This brought all kinds of terrible memories back into the open. Stanley felt himself sinking into depression. Dr. O'Donnel prescribed an antidepressant to help him with his ongoing emotional difficulties.

Stanley could not say precisely when things started to turn around, but at some point he began to notice that his journal had changed. For the first three years his journal had looked like a battle zone. The handwriting changed constantly as his different personality states used the journal to yell, blame, express frustration, and criticize each other. But more and more, the journal entries began looking like thoughtful conversations. It seemed like his personalities were using the journal not just to speak their individual minds but to listen to one another. For the first time in years his head felt quieter, like a pitching, foaming ocean had settled into a rolling, lapping sea. Six years after therapy began, Stanley felt like he had achieved enough cooperation between the different parts of himself to begin living a normal life again. Psychiatric drugs had helped make the process easier, but they could not provide the whole answer.

GLOSSARY

stigma: A public mark of disgrace, disapproval, or reproach.

Although Stanley was an adult, the drawing and words he wrote came from "Danny," the traumatized child inside him.

A CASE STUDY OF DEPERSONALIZATION DISORDER

Marion was raped when she was sixteen. She never told anyone about it; she tried to pretend it never happened. For a long time she didn't go out on dates or talk with boys her age. Finally, by the time she was in college, she felt like she could move on with her life. She was in a new state and making new friends. College felt like a place where she could start over again. She began to enjoy going out and started to remember what having fun felt like.

Marion hadn't been thinking about the rape the night her first "out of body experience" happened. She was at a party with her friends. The DJ was playing dance music and strobe lights flashed. A group of guys sidled over to her and her friends. Everyone started dancing. The guy she was dancing with was tall with blond hair. She looked up into his face and had the strangest feeling, as though she were watching him from far away. She saw her hands float up to his shoulders, but they didn't feel like her hands; instead, it was like she was watching her hands from across the room. From her distant point on the wall, she could see she was dancing to the music, but she didn't feel like she was moving at all. When she and her friends went home that night, she told them about her strange experience. They laughed and said she had too much beer. Outwardly, she laughed with them, but inside she felt disturbed. She hadn't had any beer.

Nothing more happened until two months later. Marion had just started dating a guy from her geology class. She really liked him; he was the sweetest, gentlest guy she had ever met. And yet, sometimes when they talked, she felt like she just wasn't there, as though her body were working mechanically while she sat back somewhere deep in her mind and watched. And she had strange physical sensations, too. The first time Marion's boyfriend kissed her, her lips went numb. One time they had been watching a movie. Her boyfriend was running his fingers through her hair. He suddenly stopped and gasped. She looked at him, confused, and saw he was looking at her hand. She looked down at her fist in her lap. Three red droplets oozed out between her fingers. When she opened her palm she saw she had been squeezing her fist so tightly that her fingernails had made her bleed. Strangely, though, the red crescents in her skin didn't hurt at all.

Marion finally decided to see the school physician about her strange symptoms. She told him about the numbness, lack of pain, and feelings of standing outside of her body. She said she was starting to be afraid that maybe she was really sick. Maybe she had a brain tumor or something that was making her body go numb. The doctor listened, smiled, and said that there were probably other explanations for the symptoms she was describing. He asked her if she could tell him about the types of things that had been going on in her life before the symptoms started. Before she knew what was happening, she was telling him about how she had been raped. As she talked, she again felt far away, like she was telling a story about something that happened to someone else.

After that appointment, Marion began seeing a school counselor who talked to her about depersonalization disorder. The counselor told Marion that acknowledging, grieving, and healing from what had happened to her in the past could help her stop having these disturbing symptoms in the present. Together, they worked on ways to help Marion keep from emotionally withdrawing. Sometimes, when Marion felt herself beginning to slip away, she would pick an object and stare at it intensely. She found that by examining and tracing every detail of the object she could keep herself in the present rather than slip into the distance. Marion also discussed her needs and discomforts with her boyfriend. Together, they tried to work through difficult situations.

Marion kept a journal, which she called her "distance journal." When she was having moments of depersonalization, she would open her journal and describe every aspect of the experience in detail. In therapy, she and her counselor would go through the journal and look for similarities between the depersonalization episodes to identify things that triggered the episodes and things that helped them subside. Marion's boyfriend was understanding and longed to be helpful, but eventually Marion decided she needed more time to work through her past before she could have a romantic relationship. Though she felt a deep loss when ending her relationship, she knew that she was taking the right steps toward permanently healing.

The school counselor and the doctor worked together to help Marion. They decided that an antianxiety medication would help Marion cope with her fears as she faced the reality of her rape. Marion took the medication for almost a year, and then she felt strong enough to face life without the drug's help. Again, a psychiatric drug helped her but it did not provide the whole answer.

A person with a dissociative disorder may present one personality to the world, while hiding another personality inside.

6 | Risks and Side Effects

Jason is nineteen years old and has dissociative identity disorder. He suffers from extremely high anxiety and finds that social situations like parties send him into dissociative states. He would like to take medication to help him with his anxiety, but is finding that one of his alters is creating a problem. In a therapy session, he told his psychiatrist about his concerns. He said:

> When I was younger, Roger got me through everything. It was like, whenever anything bad started to happen, I could step back and Roger would take over. He used to only come out if my dad was around, but then Roger started doing other stuff too, like getting into fights on the school bus—which was bad—and taking my math tests—which was good. I could tell that other kids thought it was weird. I mean, none of them knew it was Roger, but I could tell that they thought it was weird that I'd be so scared and quiet one minute and picking fights the next.

When a person has DID, one personality may be comfortable drinking alcohol while another is not.

When I was seventeen, I started noticing girls. Well, I'd noticed them before, of course, but now I wanted to talk to them so badly, but I'd get so scared that I'd be sick. Not just faking it either. I would really get sick. My hands would sweat, and I'd get feverish and nauseous and couldn't breathe. I wasn't going to go to my prom, but then my mom asked our neighbor's daughter if she would go with me. Getting ready that night, I was so sick I thought I would die. The last thing I remember from prom night is straightening my tie in the mirror. I started staring at myself, like I was hypnotized almost, and then I just blacked out.

The next day when I saw her, she smiled at me and called me Roger. She said I'd told her to call me that at the prom. That's how I started to figure out what was happening. Roger decided to take over talking to girls because I was so scared. And Roger was really good at it! He started smoking and drinking, trying to get into bars even though I'm under age. Roger is twenty-five and can do anything. He can't stand it that I'm under age.

Now I want to take this medication that I think could really help me be more comfortable around people, but I can't mix it with alcohol. Roger doesn't want to give up drinking. I try to explain to him that if I'm on medication, then he's on medication too and that what's bad for me is also bad for him. I think he knows, but he doesn't want to be like me—scared all the time and unable to think. He can't stand that I'm the one in control, and right now, I don't think I can trust him to cooperate.

DISCUSSION

When considering medication as a supplement to proper psychotherapeutic treatment, one must keep in mind that the effects of medication on patients with dissociative disorders can be very unpredictable. These drugs are designed to chemically influence the physical working of the brain, which means these drugs are very helpful for people with chemical imbalances. Chemical imbalances or physical conditions, however, do not cause dissociative disorders. Instead, dissociative disorders are psychologically based, and though trauma may cause chemical changes in the brain, drug intervention may have no effect on the psychological condition. Additionally, for people with DID, it is not uncommon for different personalities within the same patient to have different reactions to the prescribed medication. One personality, for example, may find the medication extremely helpful, while another personality may suffer from severe side effects like nausea and fatigue.

Of additional concern is the fact that some psychiatric drugs cause or mimic dissociative symptoms. For a person with a dissociative disorder, such medications can be extremely harmful. For example, a doctor may prescribe an anxiety-reducing medication to allow the dissociative patient to relax and sleep better. The patient's anxiety and sleeplessness are caused, however, by her dissociative experiences. If the medication causes further dissociation, it might simply make her condition worse instead of relieving her anxiety.

Specific medications carry their own individual risks as well. The class of antidepressants called MAOIs, or monoamine oxidase inhibitors, is not in most cases recommended for treating the depression of people with dissociative disorders. The main reason for limiting MAOI use is that there are certain important dietary restrictions a patient must adhere to when taking MAOIs. If the patient is suffering from episodes of amnesia, fugue states, or personality switches, he may not have enough conscious control of his actions to ensure safe adherence to the dietary restrictions.

Medication may not help the anxiety experienced by a person with a dissociative disorder.

Jason is afraid that this might happen to him. He knows that the medication could help him, but he cannot currently control when Roger takes control. Roger likes to party and be in charge. Jason does not know what he will do while he is in Roger's personality state. Roger could decide to drink alcohol or break a dietary rule, and Jason would not be able to stop him.

The problem of loss of conscious control must be carefully considered any time that medication is explored as a supplementary treatment to dissociative disorders. This problem can be even more serious if a specific personality state within the DID patient has suicidal tendencies. An un-

In some cases of DID, the person has many alternate personalities, all existing inside the same person.

stable patient with dissociative identity disorder could use the medication as a method of self-harm.

EXAMPLE

Angeline knew that she did not want to die. She had struggled so long against so much adversity, and now she was determined to get well. But not every part of her was confident about her ability to succeed.

There were always voices in her head. Martha was like an encouraging mother who said, "You can do it, Angeline. I know you're strong enough. You can make all of us well." Billy, however, was a frightened little boy. All he wanted was to be protected. His little voice spoke in the back of Angeline's mind: "Don't let them hurt me, Angeline. Keep them away." Meanwhile, Penny was filled with rage, and her voice often spoke louder than anyone else: "I hate you, Angeline! I know you hate yourself, too. You're worthless. It's all your fault. You know it, and someday everyone will know it."

"Penny, you know that's not true," Martha would intervene. "You're saying this because you're hurt and angry. You have to trust Angeline. She can make us well."

Sometimes it was so hard for Angeline to separate what she really wanted from what these other parts were telling her to do. She thought she was taking all the right steps. She was going to therapy and support groups. Billy was beginning to relax and talk about why he was so frightened. Martha gave comfort and encouragement. But Penny's depression and self-hatred wouldn't leave her mind.

After much debate, Angeline started taking antidepressants with the hope of helping Penny. Sometimes she thought Penny was beginning to listen, cooperate, and trust. But then Penny would snap back, begin planting seeds of doubt, hiding behind her fear. One night, while Angeline

Angeline's story may sound incredible, but it is not an unusual experience among people with DID. In fact, many of us experience conflicting emotions within ourselves. People with DID just experience these conflicts to a much greater degree. Have you ever been so mad at someone you loved that you said you hated her? Inside of you, you know that you love this person. But in that angry moment, another part of you feels like it hates her. For a while, you feel divided, but eventually you get over it and have unified feelings again.

stood in the kitchen, daily medication in hand, Penny turned on them all.

At the hospital, Angeline told her psychiatrist about the frightening ordeal. "It was like someone else was controlling my hand. Penny's voice in my head was screaming at me to swallow the pills. My hand kept forcing them into my mouth as fast as I could spit them out. It was like I could control my mouth, but Penny was controlling my hand. Billy was screaming, and Martha was trying to comfort him. I kept telling myself, "I don't want to die." But Penny kept screaming back, "Yes we do!"

She ended her story saying, "I'm not suicidal, but apparently Penny is."

DISCUSSION

In a person with DID, conflicting internal parts can become so divided that they begin to seem not just like separate feelings but like separate people. In many people with DID, one part of them knows that the abuse they suffered was not their fault. Often, another part of them feels guilt, shame, and self-hatred because of the abuse. This self-loathing part often develops into a destructive personality who may be responsible for self-destructive and even suicidal acts. This is what has happened to Angeline. Part of her, the part of her who calls herself Penny, feels overwhelming guilt, anger, and shame. When considering medication, a patient and her therapist must carefully consider any personality states that might use the medication for self-harm.

Like MAOIs, benzodiazepines require certain dietary considerations like refraining from alcohol, and this may be difficult for some patients with dissociative disorders. Furthermore, these drugs can be habit forming and are not appropriate for long-term use. They are therefore most safely administered under supervision, such as in a hospital setting. They are good examples of how medications do not treat dissociative disorders but may be helpful in stabilizing a patient so that the actual psychotherapeutic treatment may begin.

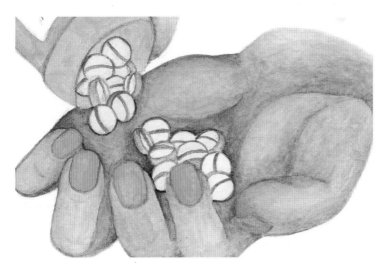

Medication does not cure dissociative disorders, but it can help stabilize the patient.

In addition to the risks certain types of medications pose to patients with dissociative disorders, there are also the risks and side effects unique to each individual medication. Everything we put into our bodies has an effect. Most things, we hope, will have a positive effect. Food gives us energy. Water *hydrates* us. Air provides oxygen to our cells. Other things can have negative effects. Eating peanuts can give energy to one person but can be fatal to a person with a severe peanut allergy. One person may swallow chlorinated water while swimming and feel fine. Another person may swallow the same amount of water and feel sick. Medications also have both positive and negative effects. Some people may experience only positive effects of a given medication. For

---

All drugs have side effects; they cause physical reactions besides the desired effect. Usually, these side effects are relatively minor, but they may seem major to some people. Side effects for antidepressants include the following symptoms:

Drug Category	Side Effect
SSRIs	usually very few side effects, but some people notice fatigue, decreased sexual drive, changes in sleep pattern, or gastrointestinal upset
TCAs	weight gain, dry mouth, diarrhea, sweating, low blood pressure, changes in heartbeat
MAOIs	weight gain, dry mouth, insomnia, decreased sexual response, and low blood pressure

Drug Approval

Before a drug can be marketed in the United States, it must be officially approved by the Food and Drug Administration (FDA). Today's FDA is the primary consumer protection agency in the United States. Operating under the authority given it by the government, and guided by laws established throughout the twentieth century, the FDA has established a rigorous drug approval process that verifies the safety, effectiveness, and accuracy of labeling for any drug marketed in the United States.

While the United States has the FDA for the approval and regulation of drugs and medical devices, Canada has a similar organization called the Therapeutic Product Directorate (TPD). The TPD is a division of Health Canada, the Canadian government department of health. The TPD regulates drugs, medical devices, disinfectants, and sanitizers with disinfectant claims. Some of the things that the TPD monitors are quality, effectiveness, and safety. Just as the FDA must approve new drugs in the United States, the TPD must approve new drugs in Canada before those drugs can enter the market.

other people, the negative effects may be so severe that they outweigh any positive gains.

There is a great range of side effects for psychiatric drugs. They can cause anything from nausea and sleeplessness to severe neurological dysfunctions like seizures. Some of the most common side effects of antidepressants are anxiety, insomnia, and weight gain. Many antianxiety drugs can cause chemical dependence. Many mood stabilizers cause fatigue. The risks and side effects associated with each particular psychiatric drug can be found in *The Physicians' Desk Reference*.

Children aren't the only ones who may be comforted by a teddy bear!

7 | Alternative and Supplementary Treatments

Derek felt stupid walking into the toy store. He flipped up the collar of his leather jacket and tried to hide his face. He avoided the gaze of the young mother pushing a stroller down the aisle. He was sixteen, for crying out loud! All the other guys his age were out learning to drive and acting tough for the girls—and he was in a toy store looking for a teddy bear. He felt like an idiot. He contemplated turning around and going right back to the parking lot where his mom was waiting in the car. This was way too embarrassing to do in front of someone else, so he had told her to stay outside.

His therapist was the one who had suggested he get a teddy bear. Outwardly, Derek had scoffed. "What would I do with a teddy bear?" he snorted. But somewhere inside of him he felt a little spark of joy. He knew part of him loved the idea of having a teddy bear, but it was just too humiliating to admit.

When his mom picked him up from the appointment he told her the absurd suggestion. "Yeah, the doctor said maybe

I should get a teddy bear," he laughed. "He said for like the times when I couldn't remember stuff. You know. That I could hold on to it. Isn't that stupid?"

His mom looked at him and smiled. "Yeah, that's pretty silly. A big guy like you with a stuffed animal." They sat silent in the car for a minute. "Then again, maybe something soft to hold on to would be kind of calming. I mean, it's not like anyone would have to know." She gave him a smile. "Maybe we'll just stop at the store on the way home, just to see."

He was absolutely mortified. And yet . . . a little part of him was happy, too. If she thought it was a good idea, well, maybe it was.

He walked down the aisle of teddy bears, peaking over his jacket collar. They were all huge and fluffy. Some had pink bows around their necks. Others were dressed up in little sailor outfits. He didn't want something huge, and he

The teddy bear offered a sense of comfort to Derek.

could definitely not have a bear that was dressed like a sailor. Then his eye fell on a little blue bear with overly big ears. He stopped. This bear? He looked it over. This weird little bear couldn't be his bear, could it? He picked it up. Yes, a little part inside of him jumped. This was it. He gave it a squeeze and headed to the checkout counter. A girl his age was working the cash register. His palms began to sweat as he handed her the bear.

"Ahh, birthday present for my little sister," he stuttered. He paid, shoved the little bear into the bag, and sprinted from the store. Back in the car, Derek refused his mother's request to see the bear. She smiled, understanding, and he began to relax. She met the funny blue bear later that evening when she found Derek curled up on the living room couch. He was fast asleep with the bear gently cradled in his arms.

DISCUSSION

Although psychiatric drugs may at times be effective supplements to therapy, other strategies also have proven benefits. Many people find it helpful to supplement their major therapy with smaller therapeutic elements that they can incorporate into their daily lives. Derek's teddy bear is an example; other examples would include doing little things like stopping for a cup of chamomile tea during the day or drawing a hot bath with lavender-scented oil after work. These strategies can do a lot to ease day-to-day stress and tension. Taking yoga and meditation classes can teach people valuable relaxation skills that can be called on in times of stress and crises. For people with dissociative disorders, a major goal of therapy is not only to deal with the traumas of the past but also to learn to handle the stresses of everyday life.

Human beings have always used art as a way to express the feelings inside of them. Sometimes people with dissociative disorders have a difficult time expressing their feelings about their past traumas because the trauma occurred when they were very young, before they had developed sophisticated verbal skills. More and more therapists are finding that art can be an important part of therapy. Patients can often draw, paint, or use other artwork to express the feelings that they don't have words for. Patients also sometimes find the things they experienced too horrible to speak aloud. Some patients find it easier to draw or paint these things than to talk about them.

Seemingly small things like comforting objects (like a teddy bear) and relaxation techniques (like deep breathing) can go a surprisingly long way in helping a person to overcome the powerful need to dissociate. Derek feels embarrassed by having something like a teddy bear. When he is away from other people, however, he finds that the teddy bear is a comfort.

Another important supplement to individual psychotherapy is often group therapy. Though most therapists would not recommend group therapy as the primary source of treatment for a person with a dissociative disorder, it can be very helpful as an additional avenue of support. Many patients with dissociative disorders feel **alienated** from other people. Their illness may cause them to feel isolated and lose friends. If their dissociation was caused by abuse from a family member, as in many cases it is, they may be **estranged** from their own families. In group therapy, patients can meet other people who are experiencing the same difficulties and who understand the hardships of struggling with a dissociative disorder. Patients can find other people to relate to who sympathize with their experiences. Because the people in group therapy are experiencing the same illness, patients can also be an important resource for each other, sharing

GLOSSARY

alienated: Feeling of being isolated from others, alone.

estranged: To be removed from the customary environment or associations where there has been love, friendship, affection.

Art therapy offers a way for people to confront and organize their conflicting emotions.

information on treatments, lessons they have learned, and ideas for coping.

Of course, as with any treatment, group therapy also has its risks. Some group therapies are run by trained professionals, while others are not. Some people may use group therapy as an outlet for frustration and negative feelings, turning what is meant to be positive into a negative experience. There is also the danger of becoming too reliant on the group therapy and losing the ability to cope outside of the support network. As with all treatments, a patient should research carefully before entering into a treatment program.

In recent years, there has been a great deal of excitement about a new therapy that may provide relief to people with a great variety of trauma related disorders. Eye movement desensitization and reprocessing, or EMDR, is a therapy technique in which patients are instructed to make specific eye movements while thinking about traumatic material. Rapid eye movement occurs during **REM sleep**. Scientists have also noted that brain activity is extremely high during this sleep state. It is believed that, although we may not be consciously aware of it at the time, during REM sleep our minds process enormous quantities of important information. EMDR attempts to engage a waking person's brain in the same types of processing that occur in REM sleep. The theory is that by moving the eyes in certain ways, we can stimulate connections in our brains that are not otherwise normally stimulated. Moving the eyes from right to left causes brain activity to move rapidly from one **hemisphere** to the other. According to current research, increasing brain activity while working through painful memories may assist patients in processing and working through the traumatic feelings. Therapists must be specially trained in the EMDR technique, and though many interesting and hopeful anec-

> ## Homeopathic Treatment for Psychiatric Disorders
>
> Homeopathy is a form of alternative medicine that looks at disease and disorders from a very different perspective from conventional medicine. It treats a person's entire physical and mental being, rather than dividing a patient into various symptoms and disorders. Homeopathic medicine uses tiny doses to stimulate the body's ability to heal itself. In some cases, these doses may be administered only once every few months or years. Homeopathic practitioners believe their approach offers safe, natural alternatives that can supplement or replace conventional pharmaceutical treatment for psychiatric problems. Homeopathic medicines have few side effects, unlike the strong chemicals used for psychiatric drugs.

dotes regarding EMDR success exist, controlled studies have yet to be done on the treatment's effectiveness for patients with dissociative disorders.

For some people with dissociative disorders, psychiatric medication is not an option for various reasons. An herbal or other "natural" alternatives may be appropriate instead. Keep in mind, though, that these "natural drugs" are still drugs; they contain chemicals that affect the body. For instance, some people who experience depression and anxiety as a part of their dissociative disorder may try an herb called Saint-John's-wort.

Saint-John's-wort has been used for many centuries in Greece, China, Europe, and North America for treating both physical and mental illnesses. Studies in Europe have found Saint-John's-wort to be very effective in treating depression

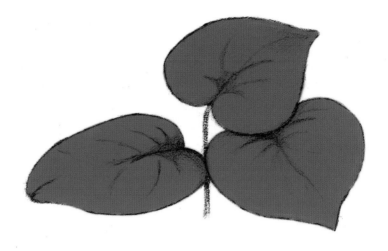

Kava leaves.

and anxiety, but the Food and Drug Administration of the United States has not approved it for such treatments. Though it can be purchased over the counter in health food, grocery, and drug stores, one should still do careful research before beginning any medicinal regimen. Herbs, even though they are natural remedies, can still have powerful effects on the body and can interact with other medications.

As of 1994, herbs like Saint-John's-wort are legally considered to be "food supplements." This means that they cannot be removed from the market as easily as if they were classified as drugs. A food supplement has to be determined to be truly dangerous before it can be removed from stores, while drugs have a lower threshold for being taken off the market.

Kava, like Saint-John's-wort, is another herb that has been used to treat depression and anxiety. Kava is a member of the pepper family and grows in the South Pacific islands. Kava root seems to have a calming effect on the mind. It is also used as a muscle relaxant for the body. In European studies, kava root was said to have the beneficial properties of benzodiazepines without the negative side effects. In very high doses, however, kava may have side effects of its own, including sleepiness and skin irritation. Like Saint-John's-wort, it can be purchased over the counter but has not been approved for medicinal use by the Food and Drug Administration.

Valerian is yet another herb that has been used for centuries both as a sleep aid and as a temporary remedy for anxiety. It seems to act as a sedative, but as with most herbal remedies, it is not approved by the Food and Drug Administration for medicinal use.

There are many other herbal remedies for conditions like depression and anxiety. You can find more information on them at your local library. Many people, however, are able to obtain relief by making simple but significant

Valerian leaves.

There are many steps that lead to emotional and physical well-being.

lifestyle changes. There are many options a person has before resorting to drugs and complicated herbal remedies. If depression, anxiety, and other difficulties plague you, look at your lifestyle first. Do you get a proper amount of sleep? Do you get that sleep at appropriate times (from 10 P.M. to 6 A.M. versus 3 A.M. to 1 P.M.)? Do you eat a healthy diet that is rich in fruits and vegetables and low in fats and sugars? Do you exercise regularly and spend some time outdoors every day? Sometimes the smallest first steps are the most important ones in changing our lives.

FURTHER READING

Allen, Thomas E., Lee Crandall Park, Mayer C. Liebman, and William C. Wimmer. *A Primer on Mental Disorders: A Guide for Educators, Families, and Students*. Lanham, Md.: Scarecrow Press, 2001.

Cavaciuti, Susan. *Someone Hurt Me*. New York: Enhancement Books, 2001.

Chu, James A. *Rebuilding Shattered Lives: The Responsible Treatment of Complex Post-traumatic and Dissociative Disorders*. New York: John Wiley and Sons, 1998.

Coffey, Rebecca. *Unspeakable Truths and Happy Endings: Human Cruelty and the New Trauma Therapy*. Lutheran, Md.: Sidran Press, 1998.

Cohen, Barry M., W. Giller, Esther Giller, and Lynn W. *Multiple Personality Disorder from the Inside Out*. Lutheran, Md.: Sidran Press, 1991.

Griffith, H. Winter, Daniel Levinson, and Miriam L. Levinson. *Complete Guide to Psychotherapy Drugs and Psychological Disorders*. New York: The Body Press/Perigee Books, 1997.

Haddock, Deborah Bray. *The Dissociative Identity Disorder Sourcebook*. New York: Contemporary Books, 2001.

Mindell, Earl, and Virginia Hopkins. *Prescription Alternatives*. New Canaan, Conn.: Keats, 1998.

Nathan, Peter E., Jack M. Gorman, and Neil J. Salkind. *Treating Mental Disorders: A Guide to What Works*. New York: Oxford University Press, 1999.

Silberg, Joyanna, L. *The Dissociative Child: Diagnosis, Treatment, and Management*. Lutheran, Md.: Sidran Press, 1998.

Spiegel, David. *Dissociative Disorders: A Clinical Review*. Lutheran, Md.: Sidran Press, 1996.

Spira, James L., and Irvin D. Yalom. *Treating Dissociative Identity Disorder*. San Franciso: Jossey-Bass, 1996.

Steinberg, Marlene, and Maxine Schnall. *Stranger in the Mirror: Dissociation: The Hidden Epidemic*. New York: Cliff Street Books, 2000.

West, Cameron. *First Person Plural: My Life as a Multiple*. New York: Hyperion, 1999.

FOR MORE INFORMATION

AtHealth.com
www.athealth.com/Consumer/disorders/Dissociative.html

Diagnosing Trauma-Related Disorders
www.rossinst.com/dddquest.htm

The International Society for the Study of Dissociation
www.issd.org/

Mental Health Matters
www.mental-health-matters.com/disorders/dissociative.php

National Alliance for the Mentally Ill
www.nami.org/helpline/dissoc.htm

Sidran Foundation and Press
www.sidran.org

Publisher's Note:

The Web sites listed on this page were active at the time of publication. The publisher is not responsible for Web sites that have changed their address or discontinued operation since the date of publication. The publisher will review and update the Web sites upon each reprint.

INDEX

BIOGRAPHIES

Autumn Libal is a graduate of Smith College and works as a free-lance writer and illustrator in northeastern Pennsylvania.

Mary Ann Johnson is a licensed child and adolescent clinical nurse specialist and a family psychiatric nurse practitioner in the state of Massachusetts. She completed her psychotherapy training at Cambridge Hospital and her psychopharmacology training at Massachusetts General Hospital. She is the director of clinical trials in the pediatric psychopharmacology research unit at Massachusetts General Hospital and has a private practice in psychopharmacology.

Donald Esherick has spent seventeen years working in the pharmaceutical industry and is currently an associate director of Worldwide Regulatory Affairs with Wyeth Research in Philadelphia, Pennsylvania. He specializes in the chemistry section (manufacture and testing) of investigational and marketed drugs.